Using Prediction Uncertainty Analysis to Design Hydrologic Monitoring Networks: Example Applications from the Great Lakes Water Availability Pilot Project

By Michael N. Fienen, John E. Doherty, Randall J. Hunt, and Howard W. Reeves

National Water Availability and Use Pilot Program

Scientific Investigations Report 2010–5159

U.S. Department of the Interior
U.S. Geological Survey

U.S. Department of the Interior
KEN SALAZAR, Secretary

U.S. Geological Survey
Marcia K. McNutt, Director

U.S. Geological Survey, Reston, Virginia 2010

For product and ordering information:
World Wide Web: http://www.usgs.gov/pubprod
Telephone: 1-888-ASK-USGS

For more information on the USGS—the Federal source for science about the Earth, its natural and living resources, natural hazards, and the environment:
World Wide Web: http://www.usgs.gov
Telephone: 1-888-ASK-USGS

Suggested citation:
Fienen, M.N., Doherty, J.E., Hunt, R.J., and Reeves, H.W., 2010, Using Prediction Uncertainty Analysis to Design Hydrologic Monitoring Networks: Example Applications from the Great Lakes Water Availability Pilot Project: U.S. Geological Survey Scientific Investigations Report 2010–5159, 44 p. [http://pubs.usgs.gov/sir/2010/5159]

Contents

Figures

Tables

Conversion Factors

Multiply	By	To obtain
foot (ft)	0.3048	meter (m)
gallon per minute (gal/min)	0.06309	liter per second (L/s)
cubic foot per second (ft^3/s)	0.02832	cubic meter per second (m^3/s)

Temperature in degrees Fahrenheit (°F) may be converted to degrees Celsius (°C) as follows:
$$°C = (°F - 32)/1.8$$

Using Prediction Uncertainty Analysis to Design Hydrologic Monitoring Networks: Example Applications from the Great Lakes Water Availability Pilot Project

By Michael N. Fienen, John E. Doherty[1], Randall J. Hunt, and Howard W. Reeves

Abstract

The importance of monitoring networks for resource-management decisions is becoming more recognized, in both theory and application. Quantitative computer models provide a science-based framework to evaluate the efficacy and efficiency of existing and possible future monitoring networks. In the study described herein, two suites of tools were used to evaluate the worth of new data for specific predictions, which in turn can support efficient use of resources needed to construct a monitoring network. The approach evaluates the uncertainty of a model prediction and, by using linear propagation of uncertainty, estimates how much uncertainty could be reduced if the model were calibrated with addition information (increased *a priori* knowledge of parameter values or new observations). The theoretical underpinnings of the two suites of tools addressing this technique are compared, and their application to a hypothetical model based on a local model inset into the Great Lakes Water Availability Pilot model are described. Results show that meaningful guidance for monitoring network design can be obtained by using the methods explored. The validity of this guidance depends substantially on the parameterization as well; hence, parameterization must be considered not only when designing the parameter-estimation paradigm but also—importantly—when designing the prediction-uncertainty paradigm.

[1] Watermark Numerical Computing and Australian National Centre for Groundwater Research and Training

Introduction

When designing groundwater monitoring and modeling programs to support resource management, hydrogeologists are faced with choices about what kind of monitoring network can most efficiently support the management decisions needed. The network of data is constrained by factors such as budget and access. In fact, budget and access can become such a central focus of the management effort that their importance for modeling can become primary. The end result is a model that is simply calibrated to "available data" and then applied to a prediction of interest, regardless of how well suited the model is for the prediction. An alternative approach is to formally assess the value of each type and location of potential calibration datum in a proposed or existing monitoring network for enhancing the certainty of specific predictions to be made by the model. Constraints such as cost and access can either be incorporated into the calculations or be considered separately.

Network design that is based on the specific predictions needed for specific management questions can help realize the greatest value from limited resources available on a project because possible locations and types of field data can be quantitatively compared and ranked. In this context, although the uncertainty of a prediction is quantified, the focus of the analysis is the *difference* in uncertainty with or without certain knowledge (for example, knowledge about likely parameter values prior to model calibration, or the collection of calibration data). This difference, in turn, indicates the relative worth a certain piece of knowledge (data) contains for the prediction of interest.

Data worth can be calculated either through the addition or subtraction of potential information (Beven, 1993). The information resulting from these two broad approaches is different and, in this report, we focus on the addition of potential information. This approach is most applicable to early stages of an investigation. Moreover, subtracting established locations from a monitoring network is expected to be a less common occurrence: collection of data at existing sites may have unanticipated future value as predictions of interest change; thus, these data may be worthwhile to retain even if of negligible value for a current prediction.

A synthetic model, based on a local inset model constructed using properties from the Lake Michigan Basin (Hoard, 2010), is used to demonstrate this analysis. Two predictions are considered: a head prediction and a flux prediction. Both predictions are made in response to the placement of a new stress—a high-capacity pumping well—near a headwater stream. The predictions are meant to represent the evaluation of ecological low flows in the stream and the impact due to operation of a new well. Monitoring for this type of impact is expected to be of increasing interest as urban development and water use increase.

An important aspect of designing the model is deciding the structure and number of parameters used to represent unknown natural-world input values to the model (Hunt and others, 2007). Parameterization can have important ramifications for the model's ability to receive the information of the calibration dataset and, thus, the model's ability to simulate the system. Parameterization can also affect the determination of data worth obtainable with that model. The example used in this study involves refinement of surface-water features in a detailed local model inset within a very large regional model. In such a case, finer discretization (relative to the regional model) and the more detailed representation of streams enhances representation of groundwater/surface-water interaction. However, generating a local model also creates an opportunity to refine the level of parameterization. Indeed, local system detail that is unimportant and simplified on the regional scale commonly becomes important on

the local scale. Moreover, the opportunity to refine parameterization provides an excellent chance to use network-design tools to determine how best to prepare the new model for its decision-making purpose. Thus, we discuss various parameterization options in the context of exploring their impact on network-design decisions.

Purpose and Scope

The purposes of this report are (1) to evaluate the results of data worth and network-analysis design by using publicly available tools and (2) to explore several scenarios in a realistic modeling context reflecting decisions supporting the early stages of a network-design application. Two main suites of tools are currently available to practitioners to make the calculations required for this type of analysis. A prediction uncertainty tool, OPR-PPR (Tonkin and others, 2007), is designed for overdetermined problems and intended to be used with the applications JUPITER (Banta and others, 2006) and UCODE_2005 (Poeter and others, 2005). Tonkin and others (2008) indicate that extension to highly parameterized problems is straightforward, although this has not previously been tested (M.C. Hill, written comm., 2009). A second software suite, PEST (Doherty, 2008a,b), is extensible to highly parameterized, underdetermined problems, including those implemented with regularization. The prediction uncertainty tools PREDUNC and PREDVAR are incorporated into the PEST suite.

Herein, we document the theoretical and practical background underlying these two approaches and demonstrate the analysis of network design by use of PREDUNC. A key element of this work is exploring the impact of parameterization strategy on network design; hence, a tool capable of investigating a range of parameterization strategies, ranging from overdetermined to underdetermined, was required. As a result, it was necessary to use PREDUNC to accomplish all goals of the analysis.

The scope of this report is confined to exploration of data worth for a network of potential head observations in the context of a head prediction and a flux prediction. The predictions are made when a high-capacity pumping well is added to the model near the headwaters of a small stream. The choice of this particular example does not preclude the use of these techniques on other types of predictions and models; indeed, both the PEST suite and OPR-PPR are model-independent by design.

Methods

Using Prediction Uncertainty for Network Design

Two main strategies can be employed to evaluate the worth of a particular piece of information: the information can be added to a base-calibration case (or to a completely uncalibrated model if at the beginning of a project), or the information can be subtracted from an existing network. For example:

Addition. *Observations can be added* to the calibration data set. The calculated uncertainty of the prediction with the new observations added will typically be less than or equal to the uncertainty without the new observations.

Addition. *Better precalibration information can be obtained* for model parameters and, again, the calculated prediction uncertainty will typically be less than or equal to the uncertainty without the new parameter information.

Subtraction. *Observations can be excluded* from an existing calibration data set, and the prediction uncertainty will typically be greater than or equal to the uncertainty with all observations included. Such an operation would be useful if one is trying to decide how to shrink an existing network with the least adverse effect on predictions of interest.

In the first example, when potential observations are added to the problem, the worth of each new addition (which can be an individual observation or a group of observations) is calculated independently from each other addition. In this report, the base case is considered to be the model with no calibration data available. Each potential observation is added individually, and its data worth is assessed. This approach is most appropriate at the beginning of a

project, where a model has been created but no observations have been identified. At this phase, the design of a monitoring strategy can be assisted by the techniques outlined herein.

The second example is focused on parameters rather than observations, and the problem is reduced to examining different types of parameters rather than the spatial distribution of parameters or inclusion of other system processes. In this way, general information about parameter information by type (for example, horizontal hydraulic conductivity in a single layer versus better constraining of recharge or streambed conductance) can guide further exploration of parameter information, such as proposing aquifer tests or recharge studies.

The third example, in which potential observations are subtracted, may seem redundant; however, these approaches are not symmetric. The third method is appropriate when trimming an existing or proposed monitoring network; for example, in response to budget constraints or transition to a new phase of work requiring different (less) monitoring.

Prediction uncertainty in PEST and OPR-PPR after the addition or subtraction of information is calculated through first-order second moment analysis (Dettinger and Wilson, 1981; Kunstmann and others, 2002; Glasgow and others, 2003). By expanding the calibration problem in a first-order Taylor series, it is assumed that the system response is sufficiently linear over the range of parameters evaluated that the linearized (Taylor expansion) representation is accurate, and the uncertainty of the prediction with or without the information being evaluated can be calculated by using linear uncertainty propagation theory. The difference in uncertainty with or without the information being evaluated leads to an assessment of worth of that information.

Sources of Uncertainty in a Bayesian Framework

A major theoretical difference between PREDUNC and OPR-PPR is that the former is derived in a Bayesian framework (appendix 1) whereas OPR-PPR is derived in the context of traditional, overdetermined regression (appendix 2).

The Bayesian conditioning framework formally includes two primary sources of uncertainty: *a priori* and epistemic. The *a priori* uncertainty is estimated before calibration and pertains to the parameters being estimated. Epistemic uncertainty also is estimated before calibration but pertains to the observations. Epistemic uncertainty is expressed in both OPR-PPR and PREDUNC through observations weights, whereas *a priori* uncertainty is supplied to OPR-PPR through prior-information equations and to PREDUNC through the explicit definition of a parameter uncertainty matrix. Both types of uncertainty are considered in the posterior estimates of parameter and prediction uncertainty. Further details of the Bayesian framework are given in appendix 1, and the two main sources of uncertainty are discussed in detail below by using the OPR-PPR and PREDUNC contexts.

A Priori Parameter Uncertainty

The PREDUNC prediction uncertainty calculation utility in PEST is derived in a Bayesian conditioning framework (see, for example, Christensen and Doherty, 2008, and appendix 1 of this report). As a result, an important component of the calculations is the *a priori* uncertainty (also referred to as the "inherent variability" or "aleatory uncertainty" (Beven, 2009, p. 24)) of the parameter field. Inherent parameter uncertainty of this type cannot be reduced, although estimates of it can decrease in response to improved knowledge about the system properties and parameters. It is also impossible to fully know the exact nature and magnitude of this uncertainty, but it can be characterized and expressed in several ways.

This uncertainty can be expressed as a full covariance matrix, reflecting characteristics of the field of parameters and their interrelations; or it can be a diagonal matrix indicating that parameters are not correlated with each other. In the full covariance case, a variogram model from geostatistics is typically adopted, whereas in the diagonal case, distinct variance or standard deviation values are applied to each parameter. The matrix C_{pp} in equation 1 indicates covariance of the parameters.

The PEST suite explicitly uses a C_{pp} matrix in its calculations, whereas in OPR-PPR, inclusion of the C_{pp} matrix must be performed by defining weights on prior information of the preferred-value type (see appendix 3).

Epistemic Uncertainty

Epistemic uncertainty (see, for example, Rubin, 2003, p. 4, and Beven, 2009, p. 24) refers to the level of uncertainty in reproduction of observations in a model due to a variety of nonrandom causes including measurement error, model error, and structural/conceptual uncertainty. This term is important to distinguish from measurement error alone, which is sometimes cited in the assignment of weights. The epistemic uncertainty values are included in the $C_{\varepsilon\varepsilon}$ matrix of covariance values. Both the PEST suite and OPR-PPR accept a full covariance matrix for $C_{\varepsilon\varepsilon}$, although in practice a diagonal matrix of weights is adopted in many cases.

Epistemic uncertainty, unlike *a priori* uncertainty, can be reduced through the collection of more or better measurements, the refinement of models, or other improvements. In theory, with a model that is a perfect representation of all complexity and processes encountered in the real world, epistemic uncertainty could be reduced to zero. In practice, however, this can never be achieved.

Calculation of Prediction Uncertainty by Using PREDUNC

In the PREDUNC results shown here, an important concept is the potential difference between prediction and calibration conditions. Two broad categories of predictions can be considered. One is the prediction of a system property at a spatial location in a model at which observations are not available for calibration. For example, a network of agricultural wells may be available to calibrate a regional model, and a prediction may be desired in a region that is slated for residential development. A second, and probably more common category is the response of a system that is to be stressed. Often, models are calibrated under historical stresses but are to be used to evaluate the system response to a future stress. Examples include changes in recharge due to climate change, pumping from a newly installed well, or a change in pumping rates in an existing well.

In the remainder of this report, it is occasionally necessary to distinguish between calibration conditions and prediction conditions. "Calibration conditions" refers to the system state for which calibration is performed and does not include the stress (or change in stress) that is being investigated for the prediction. "Stressed conditions" or "predictive conditions" refers to the system state that *does* include the stress (or change in stress) of interest for the prediction. In the example of evaluating the system response to a newly installed pumping well, calibration conditions would be the model and data available without the well pumping, and prediction conditions would be the model and data available with the well pumping. If the stress is not changing but a new spatial location is being investigated (the first broad category above), calibration conditions and predictive conditions are the same.

By using these distinctions between calibration and prediction conditions, prediction uncertainty for a prediction s is calculated by PREDUNC as

$$\sigma_s^2 = \mathbf{y}^T \mathbf{C}_{pp} \mathbf{y} - \\ \mathbf{y}^T \mathbf{C}_{pp} \mathbf{X}^T \left[\mathbf{X} \mathbf{C}_{pp} \mathbf{X}^T + \mathbf{C}_{\varepsilon\varepsilon} \right]^{-1} \mathbf{X} \mathbf{C}_{pp} \mathbf{y} \quad (1)$$

where σ_s^2 is the prediction uncertainty, $\mathbf{y}$ is the sensitivity of the prediction (under predictive stress conditions—this vector includes the sensitivity of the prediction to all parameters and is a $1 \times NPAR$ vector, where $NPAR$ is the number of parameters), $\mathbf{C}_{pp}$ is the covariance matrix of inherent variability (*a priori* uncertainty) of the parameters, $\mathbf{X}$ is the Jacobian matrix ($NOBS \times NPAR$, where $NOBS$ is the number of observations) of sensitivity under calibration conditions, and $\mathbf{C}_{\varepsilon\varepsilon}$ is the covariance of epistemic uncertainty on the observations. Note that the first term depends only on the sensitivity of the prediction to the parameters and to the inherent parameter variability. As a result, this represents the precalibration component of uncertainty. The second term, which includes sensitivity of observations to parameters in the calibration dataset and the epistemic uncertainty of the observations, represents the calibration component of uncertainty. A

derivation of these equations is included in appendix 1.

Calculation of Prediction Uncertainty by Using OPR-PPR

The general approach of OPR-PPR is the same as for the PEST PREDUNC tools. However, the structure of the prediction is based on uncertainty typically calculated at the end of a linear regression. A derivation of these equations is included in appendix 2. Adopting the symbology used in this report, the prediction uncertainty for a prediction s is calculated by OPR-PPR as

$$\sigma_s^2 = s^2 \mathbf{y}^T \left(\mathbf{X}^T \mathbf{C}_{\varepsilon\varepsilon} \mathbf{X} \right)^{-1} \mathbf{y} \quad (2)$$

where σ_s^2, $\mathbf{y}$, and $\mathbf{X}$, are the same as in equation 1, s^2 is the calculated error variance, and $\mathbf{C}_{\varepsilon\varepsilon}$ is the observation weight matrix, which corresponds to $\mathbf{C}_{\varepsilon\varepsilon}$ in equation 1. In traditional regression, the role of this formulation is to quantify the uncertainty in a prediction imparted by the observation dataset and the regression process (see, for example Draper and Smith, 1966) The Jacobian matrix ($\mathbf{X}$) can be modified to include prior-information equations (Tonkin and others, 2007), and under certain circumstances, in which prior-information equations are used with preferred-value regularization, the same calculations can be made with OPR-PPR as with PREDUNC. Implementation limitations in the OPR-PPR software (version 1.00) include application to problems with relatively few parameters (on the order of 100). Further details of the derivation and implementation of OPR-PPR and a comparison with PREDUNC are given in the appendixes to this report.

Comparison of PREDUNC and OPR-PPR

One of the goals of this study was to compare the theoretical backgrounds underpinning both PREDUNC and OPR-PPR. The mathematical details are covered in depth in the appendixes to this report.

PREDUNC is derived in the context of Bayesian updating. In this way, an *a priori* estimate of inherent parameter covariance ($\mathbf{C}_{pp}$) is updated with the information added through the calibration process to a specific set of data. Regularization equations are not considered in these calculations, and no other prior information equations are required or used to make the calculations.

OPR-PPR is derived in the context of overdetermined regression. Prediction uncertainty in this context is intended to indicate the propagation of uncertainty in the observations to parameter estimates. The extension to include prior information allows inclusion of a $\mathbf{C}_{pp}$ matrix characterizing inherent parameter covariance in the form of weights on prior-information equations of the "preferred-value" type. Provided that the weights on prior-information equations correspond to $\mathbf{C}_{pp}^{-1}$, the prediction uncertainty calculations in OPR-PPR are equivalent to those in PREDUNC.

Further details of the circumstances required for PREDUNC and OPR-PPR to yield equivalent results are given in appendix 3. Programmatic limitations on the number of parameters that can be used with a combination of UCODE_2005 Version 1.015 and OPR-PPR Version 1.00 prevented a direct comparison of the results with PREDUNC. However, by using MATLAB Release R2008b (Mathworks, 2008), the results from using both forms of the equations were compared and found to be equivalent under the circumstances detailed in appendix 3. The calculations discussed in the remainder of this report were made with PREDUNC.

Model Description

The methods discussed in this report were applied to a local model inset within a groundwater/surface-water interaction model created by Hoard (2010). The model uses a telescopic mesh-refinement approach where a local model was constructed (cell size = 21.8 m) within an intermediate model (cell size = 152.4 m), which was, in turn, inset within a regional model (cell size ranging from 1,524 m to more than 21,000 m) of the Lake Michigan Basin (Feinstein and others, 2010). The purpose of the two-step insets was to explore downscaling of regional climatic conditions at the large basin scale to a scale appropriate for evaluating impacts on small streams. Local exploration of stream/aquifer interactions was another motivation

for a local model inset within an intermediate or regional model. The features and locations of the regional, intermediate and local models are shown in figure 1. The model contains six layers, of which the shallowest two are of principal interest in this investigation. Recharge and fixed-head lateral boundaries, simulated with the RCH and BAS packages within MODFLOW-2005 Version 1.6 (Harbaugh, 2005), combine with surface-water features modeled through the streamflow routing (SFR) package to represent water inflows and outflows. Further details about the model features and implementation are discussed in Hoard (2010).

Domain and General Model Characteristics

The domain of the local model is depicted in figure 2. The locations of the pumping well, the well location for a head prediction, and the streamgage location for a flux prediction also are shown. The local model was run at steady state with fixed boundaries inherited from the intermediate model (rather than being run as a fully coupled version with the local grid refinement (LGR) package (Mehl and Hill, 2005; Hoard, 2010)). The techniques could be extended to transient cases and full intermediate-to-local iterative coupling via the LGR package (with an accompanying increase in computational demands). The steady-state, non-linked approach was adopted here to keep forward model run times short (several minutes), thus enabling comparison of many different methods and assumptions.

Stress and Prediction

The calibration condition for the local model consists of recharge, the presence of streams that interact with the aquifer, and constant-head boundaries inherited from the intermediate model. No pumping wells are present in the calibration conditions. The prediction conditions include a new stress—the addition of one new pumping well, extracting at 500 gal/min from layer 2 at the location indicated in figure 2. Two predictions related to the new stress are investigated: one head in a location between the pumping well and stream (figure 2, cell H115_259 in layer 1) and one flux prediction in the

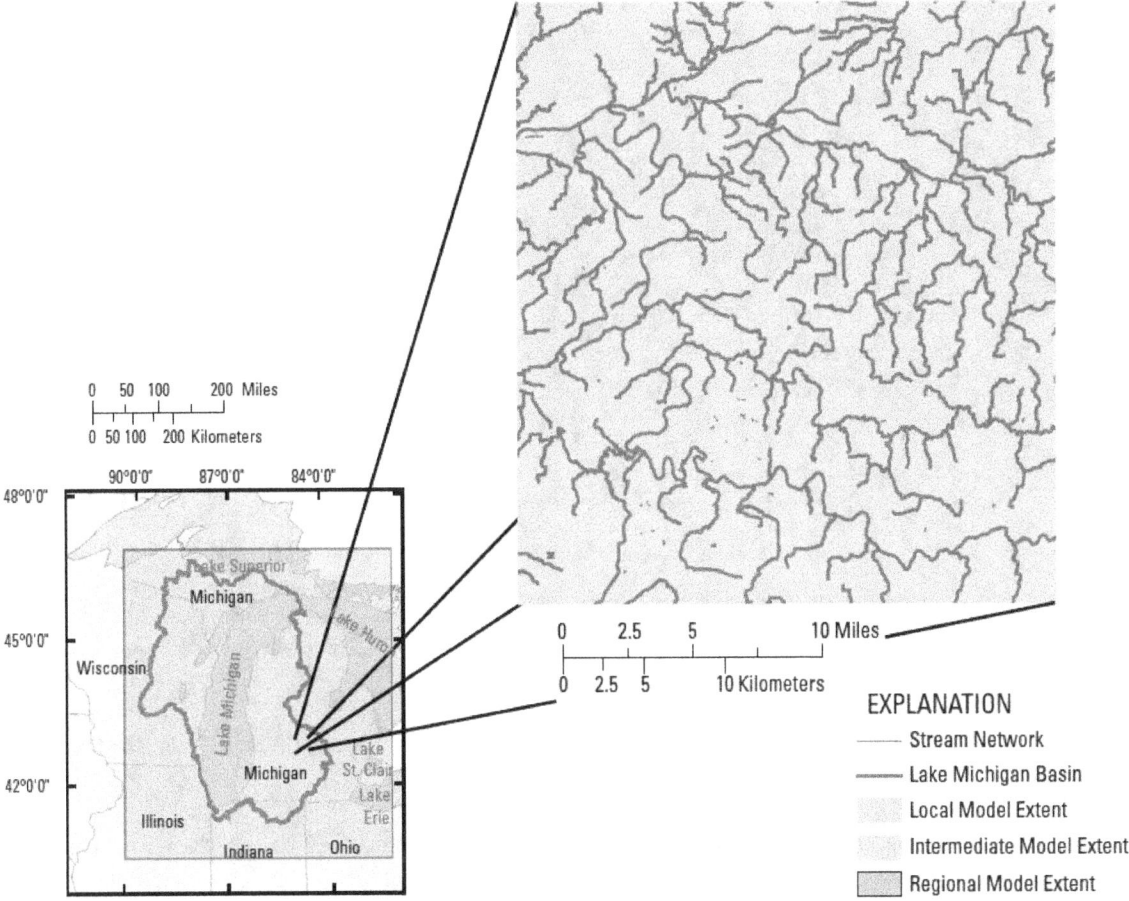

Figure 1.   The location and features of the regional, intermediate, and local models. Figure modified from Hoard (2010).

nearby stream (figure 2; named "streamgage 17"). Both predictions are intended to indicate possible ecological impacts in the stream due to installation of a moderately sized extraction well; for example, the first might be related to change in water levels in a riparian wetland and the second related to effects of pumping on flows needed for trout or other species of societal interest.

Figure 3 shows the head contours of the local model in layers 1 and 2 under the stressed conditions. A full description of the model layer geometry is given by (Hoard, 2010). The behavior of surface-water features is reasonable in these contour plots, and the effect of pumping can be seen. The characteristics of this head solution have utility for interpretation of data worth. For example, note the refracted contour lines that are most pronounced in layer 1. These are the result of hydraulic-conductivity contrasts in the zonation

inherited from the regional model.

Parameterization

Parameterization, and the simplification decisions made during parameterization, can have ramifications on predictive uncertainty (Moore and Doherty, 2005; Doherty and Hunt, 2009). In a traditional approach to parameterization, the modeler is forced to make subjective decisions to simplify the natural world to a tractable modeling problem, most commonly by using zones of piecewise constancy. Although rarely done in practice, the uncertainty associated with such decisions can be estimated by using the approaches of Cooley (2004) and Cooley and Christensen (2006). These approaches are computationally expensive, however, and not suited for directing the modeler to actions that can address unacceptable uncertainty. A highly parameterized,

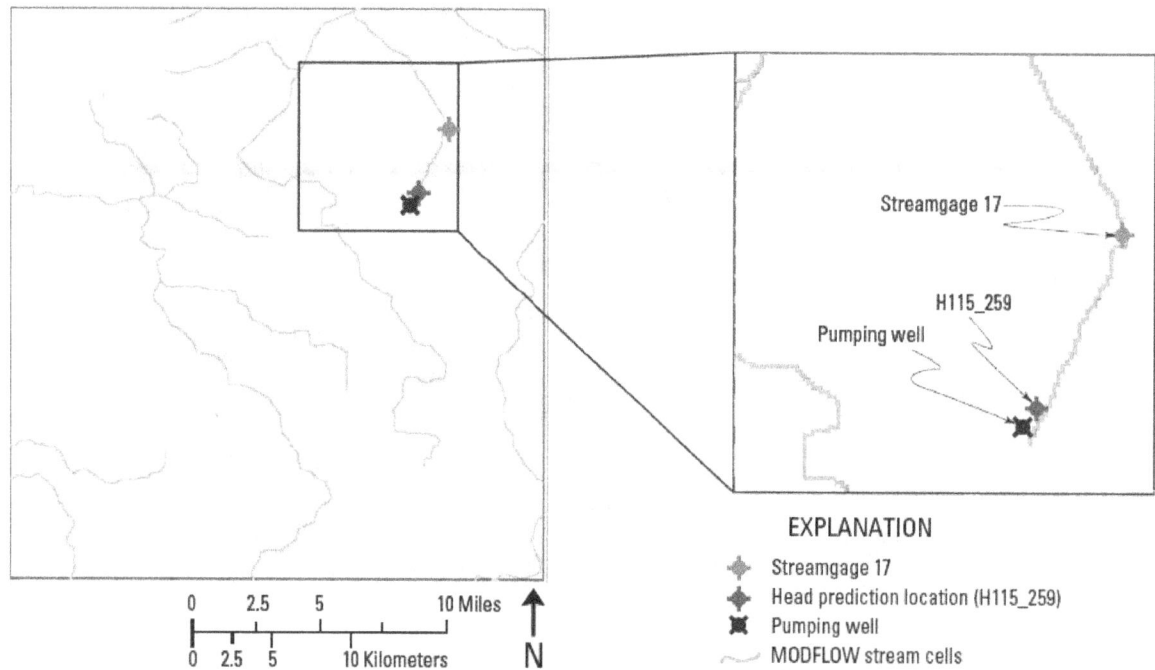

Figure 2.   Local model domain and the locations of the pumping well, the head prediction (H115_259), and the flux prediction (streamgage 17).

regularized inversion approach, on the other hand, builds the problems by using large numbers of parameters with additional mathematical techniques to constrain the additional parameters through soft knowledge of the system (Hunt and others, 2007; Doherty and Hunt, 2009). Large numbers of parameters do not necessarily mean high parameter heterogeneity, however, if the balance of soft knowledge (that is, qualitative information known about the site) and model fit is appropriate (for example, Fienen and others, 2009a,b). Rather, deviations from the preferred condition occur only when the improvement in the model fit is of sufficient magnitude to offset the deviation from the preferred condition. Such regularized inversion approaches help reduce the epistemic error component of uncertainty, which is particularly valuable when characterizing subtle aspects of data worth, such as comparing one location for a potential head measurement to another nearby potential head measurement.

To demonstrate the effect of parameterization on data-worth analyses, three parameterizations are considered (figure 4): a hydraulic conductivity (K)

layer-multiplier ("KLM") approach in which a single multiplier is applied to all horizontal and vertical hydraulic-conductivity values in each layer inherited from the regional model, yielding a 12-parameter model; a 300-parameter version of the K field ("300K") in which the zonation inherited from the regional model was used to define 300 hydraulic-conductivity parameters in the model (25 horizontal K and 25 vertical K parameters in each of the 6 model layers); and pilot-point or "PP" approach (Doherty, 2003) in which a 20×20 grid of pilot points was used to represent both horizontal and vertical hydraulic conductivity, with estimated values kriged to the model grid in areas between the pilot points. The PP approach has 4,800 parameters. To better compare the three levels of parameterization, all parameters were treated as multipliers such that their initial value is unity for all cases and uncertainty is expressed as a fraction of that initial value.

A critical aspect of this parameterization is that the model-node geometry and the parameter base values themselves underlying all the parameterizations are the same—inherited from the regional model. As a result, the impacts of

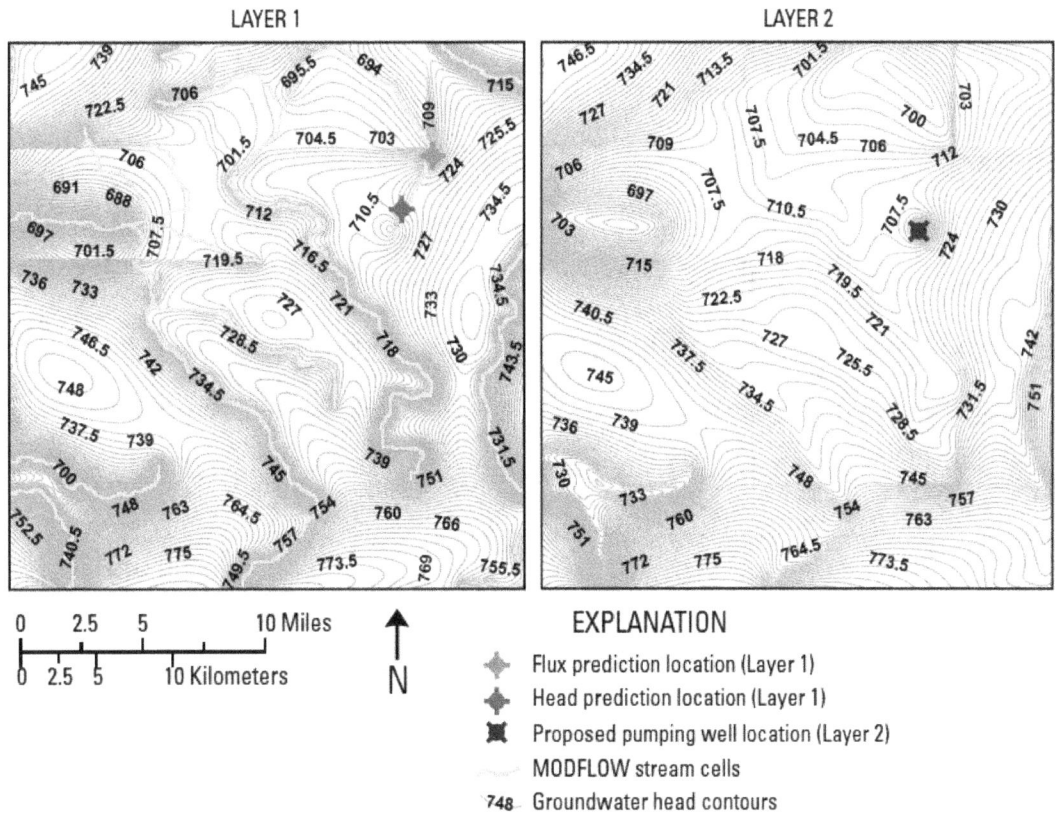

Figure 3. Head contours in layer 1 (left panel) and layer 2 (right panel). The contour interval is 1.5 feet.

parameterization enter the problem in two ways: (1) the spatial area of the domain perturbed when evaluating the Jacobian sensitivity matrix, and (2) the resolution of the *a priori* parameter uncertainty matrix (C_{pp}). These differences are shown to have a substantial impact on the results of prediction uncertainty analysis.

These three parameterizations allow investigation of different facets for using models for data worth analyses. The KLM case was chosen both to evaluate the parameter worth in a categorical sense (in other words, broad categories of parameter type rather than repeated instances distributed spatially throughout the model domain) and to serve as an extreme example of lumping as might happen in "back of the envelope" estimates of system response as simulated by a slightly modified version of the regional model where the surface water features are refined but the local aquifer properties are not. Using the KLM approach, one assumes that downscaling the major elements of the model from the intermediate scale

(for example, the stream geometry, boundary conditions, and grid resolution) will be adequate to simulate the stream and groundwater interactions in the local model. If so, the KLM version of the problem should suffice for assessing data worth. The 300K case was chosen as a moderately parameterized example in which some additional flexibility beyond the regional model is allowed in addition to the surface-water feature refinement of the KLM approach. This can be thought of as an end extreme of the number of zones that might be tried in a traditional calibration approach. The PP case represents a highly parameterized case typical of a regularized inversion approach that aims to overcome potential artifacts of parameter lumping and the associated structural error by using minimal assumptions about the geometry and lumping of the hydraulic-conductivity field. The three parameterizations are considered members along a natural continuum of model refinement.

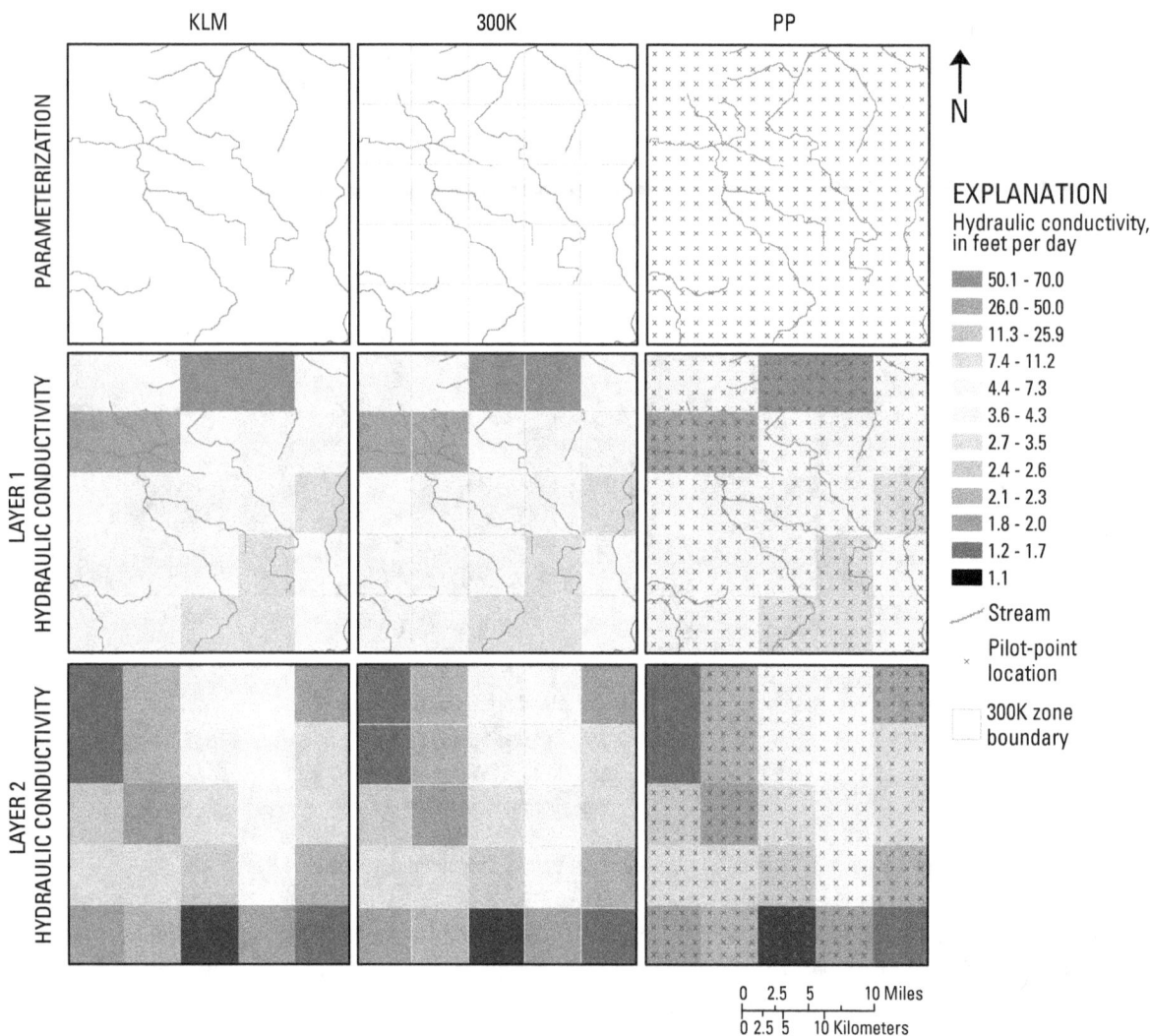

Figure 4.   Local model domain showing the parameterization and observation network. The left panel is KLM, the middle panel is 300K, and right panel is the PP (pilot points) parameterization. The grid in 300K outlines hydraulic conductivity zone boundaries; the 'x' marks on PP show the pilot point locations. The KLM, 300K, and PP parameterizations are described in the "Parameterization" section.

Observation Network

For this analysis, it is assumed that no existing data are available for the model domain beyond those used to constrain the regional model. Thus, the network of observations for this study is different from a typical calibration dataset, and observations are placed at the positions where *potential* observations might be placed rather than at the locations of existing wells. By using the concept of notional calibration (Doherty, 2008b), these observations are intended to be assessed for data worth, as described below, rather than as actual calibration targets. The network of potential observations is shown in figure 5 and is focused on the locations of both the proposed pumping well and the head and flux predictions. If existing data were included, the worth of new data would represent the incremental reduction in prediction uncertainty due to addition of the new data. The omission of a pre-existing dataset changes only the baseline of relative worth comparison and, for clarity of interpretation in this study, the baseline is assumed to be no data.

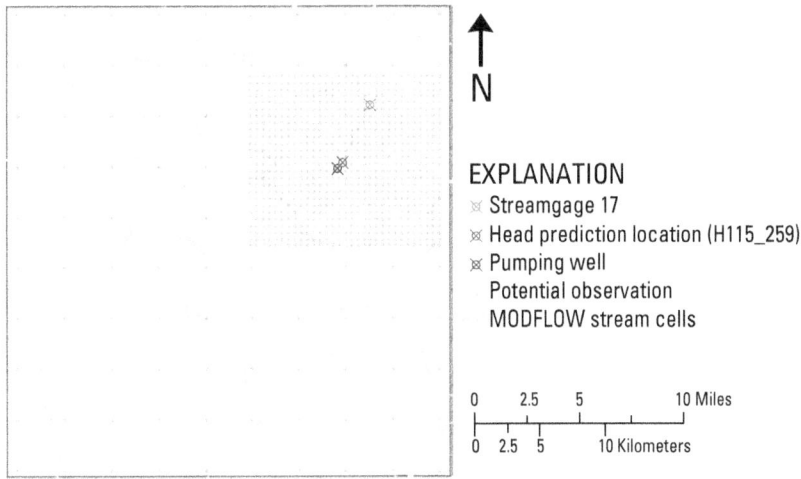

Figure 5.   Potential head observation network. The same observation network is applied to the first and second layers.

Structural Parameters

In the "Methods" section, *a priori* and epistemic uncertainty were discussed. These sources of uncertainty enter the calculations as parameters in the $\mathbf{C}_{pp}$ and $\mathbf{C}_{\varepsilon\varepsilon}$ matrices, respectively. To differentiate these parameters from the main model parameters (hydraulic conductivity, for example) the uncertainty parameters are referred to as "structural parameters." Structural parameters are not related to "structural uncertainty" as discussed later in this report—an unfortunate overlap in the prevailing terminology. Structural parameters are discussed here to indicate the means by which sources of uncertainty are introduced to the mathematics of the problem.

In this study, a diagonal matrix was adopted for $\mathbf{C}_{pp}$ in all cases. This implies an absence of correlation (and, therefore, continuity) among the parameters. Although this assumption is an approximation and not fully correct, it was adopted as a simpler approach that also could easily adopted in a real-world application. The inclusion of a full covariance matrix, if desired, is typically accomplished by using a geostatistical variogram. Scenarios with different relative uncertainty among parameter groups are investigated by changing the diagonal elements of $\mathbf{C}_{pp}$ for recharge relative to hydraulic conductivity. In the OPR-PPR framework, formal adoption of the $\mathbf{C}_{pp}$ matrix is currently infeasible because the OPR-PPR calculations are not based on Bayesian conditioning. However, it is possible to use prior-information equations to include similar information in the problem, although this is not the documented intent of such information (as discussed in appendix 3).

In all scenarios investigated in this study the same values for epistemic uncertainty are assumed. The head observation values were assumed to have an epistemic uncertainty, expressed as standard deviation, of 5 ft. The epistemic uncertainty is provided to the problem through weights on observations and, in this case, weights were set as the inverse of the standard deviation values (0.2 ft).

Parameter Contributions to Prediction Uncertainty

One approach to network design for minimizing prediction uncertainty is through obtaining more accurate information about parameters. The goal of this approach is to identify, for a given model conceptualization, which parameters have the largest impact on the uncertainty of a prediction of interest. This can be done by using the PPR approach (Tonkin and others, 2007) or by using the PREDUNC4 or PREDVAR2-4 suite of tools in PEST (Doherty, 2008a,b).

These tools allow modelers to determine which parameters contribute most to the uncertainty of a prediction of interest. Armed with this knowledge, they can decide which parameters to target for better knowledge. For example, if hydraulic conductivity is most important, the next phase of work may benefit from a pumping test to better constrain hydraulic conductivity. Similarly, if recharge is the most important, a field investigation aimed at better constraining of recharge may be a better use of limited budgets for the next phase of work. Importance is defined here as contribution to the prediction uncertainty by a specific parameter type.

In this work, PREDUNC4 was used for the analysis, whereby the prediction uncertainty is calculated with all parameters assumed known to a level of certainty indicated by $\mathbf{C}_{pp}$, and then prediction uncertainty is recalculated for each parameter with the assumption that it is perfectly known. In this way, the contribution to prediction uncertainty by each parameter can be assessed. The assignment of a specific level of uncertainty to a parameter of interest can be implemented in the PREDUNC suite of tools by recalculating prediction uncertainty with various instances of the $\mathbf{C}_{pp}$ matrix. However, this approach is not explicitly documented, and this study implements the more typical PREDUNC approach of assessing parameter worth by recalculating prediction uncertainty with assumed perfect knowledge of the parameter for comparison.

The PPR statistic (Tonkin and others, 2007, p. 10) is calculated as

$$PPR = \left[1.0 - \left(\frac{s_{z'_\ell(+j)}}{s_{z_\ell}} \right) \right] \times 100 \qquad (3)$$

where $s_{z'_\ell(+j)}$ is the prediction standard deviation calculated with increased parameter knowledge and $s_{z'_\ell}$ is the prediction standard deviation without the increased parameter knowledge. The approach to calculating the PPR statistic is different from assigning the uncertainty such that a parameter is assumed to be perfectly known.

In the remainder of this section, "importance" is characterized as the contribution to total prediction uncertainty made by each parameter. The numerical results can be thought of as

$$\text{importance} = \left(\frac{PPR}{100} - 1 \right) \times 100 \qquad (4)$$

The parameters of interest are identified in table 1 and represent the KLM parameterization discussed in the "Parameterization" section.

Table 1. Parameters for the KLM scenario investigated by using PREDUNC4 to identify which parameter groups contribute most to the prediction uncertainty.

Symbol	Description
KH1	Multiplier on horizontal hydraulic conductivity in layer 1.
KH2	Multiplier on horizontal hydraulic conductivity in layer 2.
KH3	Multiplier on horizontal hydraulic conductivity in layer 3.
KV1	Multiplier on vertical hydraulic conductivity in layer 1.
KV2	Multiplier on vertical hydraulic conductivity in layer 2.
KV3	Multiplier on vertical hydraulic conductivity in layer 3.
R	Multiplier on the entire recharge array.
SL	Multiplier on the value used for streambed leakance in all streams.

Two *a priori* uncertainty scenarios were considered. In the first, all multipliers on all parameters (table 1) were assumed to have standard deviation (σ) of 0.25 units in $\log_{10}$ space, meaning that their 90-percent confidence limits would extend over about one order of magnitude. In the second scenario, recharge was assumed to be more certain (a typical assumption in models like this one), so its uncertainty was reduced to $\sigma = 0.0625$.

Figure 6 shows the contributions of each parameter type to the head-prediction uncertainty in both *a priori* uncertainty scenarios. When *a priori* uncertainty is equal for all parameters, recharge is shown to be the most important parameter, followed by vertical hydraulic conductivity in layer 1 (the layer containing the prediction) and horizontal hydraulic conductivity in layer 2 (the layer containing the well). This outcome is consistent with what might be expected, given that recharge is important for the overall mass balance of water in the system and that the pressure must propagate vertically through layer 1 and horizontally through layer 2 to be transmitted between the pumping- and observation-well locations. However, recharge is commonly assumed to be better known than hydraulic conductivity; thus, in the case where *a priori* uncertainty on recharge is lower than for hydraulic conductivity, the relative impact on prediction uncertainty due to recharge decreases, and streambed leakance becomes more important. The relative contributions of hydraulic conductivity to one another remains unchanged, but relative to recharge, the contribution of hydraulic conductivity is increased.

The contributions of each parameter type to the flux-prediction uncertainty are shown in figure 7. In this case, the streambed leakance is more important than recharge, which follows from the fact that the streambed leakance is the main control of exchange between the stream and the groundwater system. Recharge and horizontal hydraulic conductivity in layer 1 also play important roles, but the other parameters are shown to make minimal contributions. Even when the *a priori* uncertainty of recharge is reduced, as shown in the right panel of figure 7, the relative importance of streambed leakance and KH1 remain generally unchanged. This is because recharge plays a less significant role in prediction uncertainty in flux prediction than in the head-prediction case above.

Determining Observation Locations for Reducing Prediction Uncertainty

A second approach to network design for minimizing prediction uncertainty is through obtaining more observation information. The goal of this approach is to identify which are the most influential in reducing the uncertainty of a prediction of interest. The result is assessing the "worth" of each potential observation for achieving the goal of low prediction uncertainty. This can be done by using the OPR approach (Tonkin and others, 2007) or the PREDUNC1,5 or PREDVAR1,5 suite of tools in PEST (Doherty, 2008a,b). In this study, PREDUNC5 was used for the analysis and OPR was not used because it is not extensible to the highly parameterized PP case.

As mentioned previously, there are two principal methods by which the "worth" of a specific observation can be evaluated: observations can either be added to or subtracted from the calibration process.

In the first method—where observations are added—the prediction uncertainty is first calculated without any calibration data (the first term in equation 1) and then, is sequentially recalculated after adding each potential observation. The prediction uncertainty calculated by using even a single observation to calibrate is less than or equal to the uncertainty calculated without calibration data. The metric of interest, therefore, is the decrease in uncertainty expected for each potential observation. These results can be displayed on a map to indicate general areas of the model domain where added observations will have the most impact on decreasing prediction uncertainty.

In the second method—where observations are subtracted—prediction uncertainty is initially calculated by using the entire calibration data set (using both terms of equation 1) and then, sequentially, each observation is removed from the second term and the prediction uncertainty is recalculated. There should be an increase in prediction uncertainty when each observation is removed, so the metric of interest is the increase in prediction uncertainty incurred via removal of an existing observation.

Calculation of these metrics separately may seem redundant, but they are not symmetric. In the first method, each observation is considered independently, whereas in the second method, the impact on prediction uncertainty of each observation is related to those around it. Therefore, the applications of the two methods differ. The first method is most appropriate when designing a monitoring network; where one did not previously exist. The second method is appropriate when trimming an existing or proposed monitoring network, for example in response to budget constraints or transition to a new phase of work requiring different (less) monitoring.

In this study, the metric of decrease in prediction uncertainty due to addition of observations is considered as the hypothetical situation of designing a previously nonexistent monitoring network. This situation is probably more common than reduction of an existing network, and the approach is easily adapted for the case with existing data considering decreases in prediction uncertainty relative to the baseline of the existing data rather than the baseline of no data.

For this analysis of adding observations, the relative reduction in uncertainty that would be gained

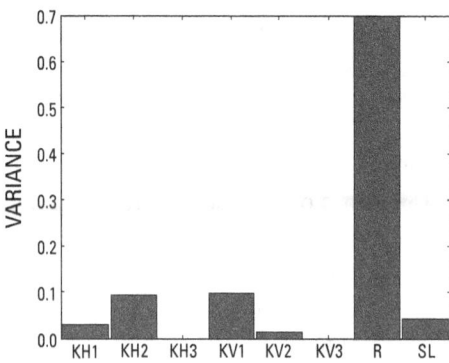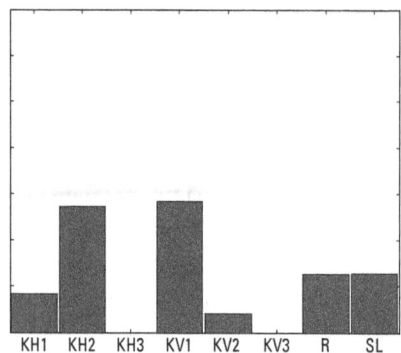

Figure 6.   Contributions of parameter groups to prediction uncertainty for a head prediction in layer 1, row 115, column 259 (fig. 2). In the left panel, *a priori* uncertainty for all parameters was set at $\sigma = 0.25$. In the right panel, recharge uncertainty was set at $\sigma = 0.0625$ while all other parameter standard-deviation values were set at $\sigma = 0.25$. See table 1 for parameter definitions.

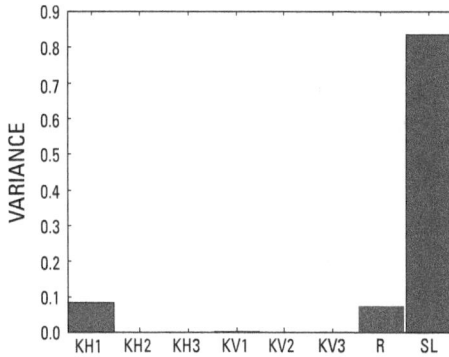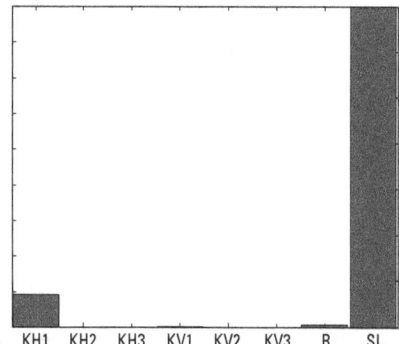

Figure 7.   Contributions of parameter groups to prediction uncertainty for a flux prediction in segment 15, reach 6 (fig. 2). In the left panel, *a priori* uncertainty for all parameters was set at $\sigma = 0.25$. In the right panel, recharge uncertainty was set at $\sigma = 0.0625$ while all other parameter standard-deviation values were set at $\sigma = 0.25$.

by adding each potential head observation in layers 1 and 2 is evaluated under two scenarios. Figure 5 shows the locations of potential head observations, which are the same for layers 1 and 2. The *a priori* uncertainty for hydraulic conductivity is set at $\sigma = 0.25$ and for recharge is set at $\sigma = 0.0625$. Subsets of this scenario are the parameterization scenarios discussed above. Specifically, each of the *a priori* uncertainty scenarios was evaluated by using the scenarios defined in the previous parameterization section as KLM, 300K, and PP.

The normalized decrease of prediction uncertainty variance for locations in the potential observation network is defined as data worth, calculated as

$$\text{data worth} = \sigma^2_{norm} = \frac{\sigma^2_{dec}}{\sigma^2_{total}} \qquad (5)$$

where σ^2_{norm} is the normalized prediction-uncertainty variance for a given observation, σ^2_{dec} is the decrease in prediction-uncertainty variance predicted if a given observation is included in the calibration, and σ^2_{total} is the total prediction-uncertainty variance. This normalization is similar to the OPR statistic defined in Tonkin and others (2007, p. 7). Note that, in the case of the OPR statistic, the sign indicates whether the observation is being added or subtracted—in this example, one may consider σ^2_{norm} as the absolute value of *OPR*.

Head-Observation Importance for a Head Prediction

Data worth, as defined in equation 5, is displayed as interpolated maps in figure 8 for the head prediction identified in figure 2. The potential observations are head observations in the network shown in figure 5. In figure 8, the differences in the displayed values from left panel to right reflect progressively more flexible parameterization of hydraulic conductivity, from a single value per layer at left (KLM) through a 5×5 grid of homogeneous zones (300K) to a 20×20 grid of pilot points (PP) at the right.

Two major trends are evident when comparing the parameterization scenarios: first, non-intuitive artifacts are encountered at the coarser KLM and 300K discretizations in areas that are distant from both the stress and the related prediction; second, in the highly parameterized PP case, appropriately higher values of data worth become evident in the general area where one would expect data worth—the area near both the stress and the prediction.

These artifacts are indicative of the confounding effects of structural uncertainty incurred by imposing sharp but ultimately arbitrary parameter boundaries in the hydraulic conductivity field. Moreover, these boundaries are often away from the area of interest. The resolution of the parameterization impacts the resolution of the Jacobian matrix used extensively in calculating the statistics. This structural uncertainty is not explicitly accounted for in the calculations of prediction uncertainty with equation 1 when a diagonal $\mathbf{C}_{pp}$ matrix is used to characterize *a priori* parameter uncertainty. A diagonal $\mathbf{C}_{pp}$ matrix implies complete statistical independence of the hydraulic conductivity parameters and is the simplest imposition of this information. The alternative is use of a variogram or other spatial covariance structure, but justifying a meaningful covariance representation is difficult for homogeneous zones (especially in the extreme case of a single homogeneous zone per layer). The cost of this structural uncertainty adversely affects the design of the potential observation network because the oversimplification of the parameters overwhelms the method's ability to discern subtle information, such as one head location versus an adjacent head location within the same zone. The effects of oversimplification caused by the hard-wired imposition of zonal boundaries can be mitigated through use of a highly parameterized approach such as pilot points, whereby more parameter flexibility is introduced and the effects of correlated structural noise are sufficiently reduced to

discern the difference in importance of potential head location.

In the PP scenario in layer 1, the location of a southwest-northeast trending stream that is nearest the stress and prediction can be seen as reducing data worth for potential head observations, as would be expected given the stream's ability to constrain the sensitivity of nearby heads (Hunt, 2002). There is asymmetry about the stream, with potential observations east of the river having greater data worth—a counterintuitive result since the prediction is on the western edge of the stream. This result indicates greater importance of the eastern part of the domain for describing the distribution of flow into stream capture and underflow captured at the well. Indeed, inspection of figure 3 shows that most flow to the pumping well originates to the east of the stream. The limited value of placing head observations in the stream, because the stream itself already provides information regarding head, is indicated by very low data-worth values in locations coincident with the stream.

In the PP scenario in both layers 1 and 2, the location for maximum data worth is collocated with a subtle groundwater divide, as indicated on the head contour map in figure 2 delineating the capture zone of the pumping well. The low values associated with potential head observation locations in the streams are absent in layer 2 in agreement with the absence of the streams themselves in layer 2.

Head-Observation Importance for a Flux Prediction

Data worth, as defined in equation 5, is displayed in figure 9 for the flux prediction identified in figure 2. The potential observations are head observations in the network shown in figure 5.

The artifacts discussed for the non-highly-parameterized scenarios KLM and 300K are present for the flux prediction, although they are less pronounced. This result is expected, given that flux predictions integrate larger parts of the model domain thus are more suited for the larger zones used in the KLM and 300K models. Moreover, this result is supported by the information in figure 7, which indicates that the most significant parameters for reducing flux prediction uncertainty are streambed

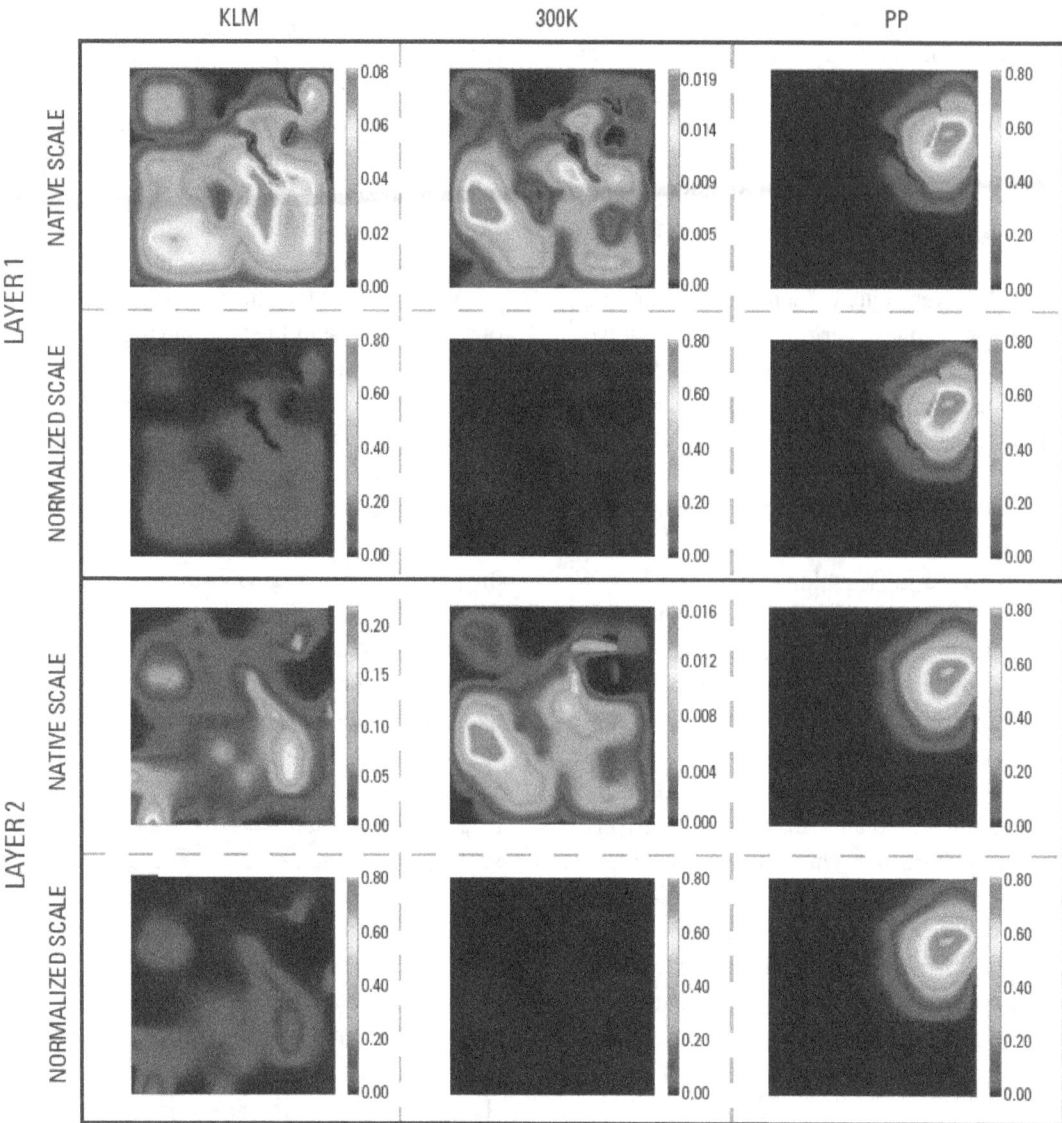

Figure 8.   Observation data worth for head-prediction scenario evaluated for layer 1 (upper 6 panels) and layer 2 (lower 6 panels). In each row of panels, three parameterizations are shown: KLM (left panel), 300K (middle panel) and PP (right panel). The values of data worth presented are normalized prediction uncertainty variance σ^2_{norm} calculated according to equation 5. Results are shown both at native scale to show detail and at a normalized scale relative to the PP results. The KLM, 300K, and PP parameterizations are described in the "Parameterization" section.

leakances. Because head observations are much more closely tied to local variability in hydraulic conductivity than streambed leakance, it is not surprising that their overall worth for prediction uncertainty would be more muted. Nonetheless, once again, the highly parameterized results provide valuable insights into the worth of head observations for the flux prediction.

The asymmetry in the worth of layer 1 head-observation data for the head prediction appears again in the context of the flux prediction. This asymmetry can also be explained by inspecting the head-contour solution in figure 3 which shows more water entering the stream from the east than the west. As a result, information about the head gradient to the east of the stream is likely to be more informative than similar information to the west.

Under pumping stress conditions, the streamgages in the region of the stream indicated by low data worth are dry, which creates the artifact of limited data worth near and upstream from them. Clearly, much information is imparted by better knowledge of the location of the interface of the dry and non-dry areas of the streams. This limitation is a drawback of the use of linear statistics for this analysis; the drying of a stream is a nonlinear (threshold) impact and therefore is not well characterized by the linear analysis.

In layer 2, the impact of the streams is muted, as it was for the head prediction. Especially notable is that the 300K parameterization implies that none of the potential head observations would be valuable for reducing prediction uncertainty on the flux prediction, but such a finding is not likely. The PP scenario results provide more valuable information in this context.

Discussion and Conclusions

A model calibration process can be enhanced (in terms of reducing uncertainty of a specific prediction to be made by a model) by obtaining either more accurate information about a parameter or more calibration data (observations). This analysis can be done at any phase of a project and is inherent to many adaptive-management scenarios. In this study, the focus is a specific scenario in which a local model with sparse local information was extracted from a calibrated intermediate model. Such a scenario may be common where a new stress too small to be seen at the regional scale (in this case, a single pumping well) is proposed in an area covered by a regional model and a refined representation of surface-water features and system properties is needed to make an accurate prediction.

The results highlight important questions that are raised in the process of creating the local model but not usually formally addressed. Is the parameterization inherited from the regional model adequate for the smaller-scale question addressed by the local model? Are the parameter values calibrated at the regional scale appropriate at the local scale? Visual inspection of figure 3 serves as a foundation for addressing these questions. The head field

behaves generally as one would expect, given the refined geometry of streams. However, significant artifacts visibly highlight the hydraulic-conductivity contrasts in the inherited hydraulic-conductivity zones. These observations suggest that the refinement of geometry in a downscaled local inset model would improve the applicability of the model, but it is likely that recalibration with data appropriate to the scale of the local model would be required.

Once the need to recalibrate the local model is established, the motivation for the modeling changes. What type of monitoring network can be designed such that the model makes the most accurate (certain) prediction? These questions can be answered by using the propagation of uncertainty, implemented in this case by use of linear methods, through a notional calibration process to determine how much the uncertainty of a prediction can be reduced by inclusion of a specific new source of data (or refined estimation of *a priori* parameter uncertainty).

Potential information on parameter *a priori* uncertainty also was evaluated by investigating broad categories. Parameter contributions to prediction uncertainty were evaluated for vertical and hydraulic conductivity of entire layers, a single multiplier on streambed conductance for all streams in the model, and a single multiplier on the recharge array. A more distributed approach for the more highly parameterized conceptualizations could be evaluated and the results contoured—this helping to ensure that the adverse effects of parameter oversimplification are reduced. However, such an analysis should be accompanied by an evaluation of support volume for parameter information, which is beyond the scope of this report. For example, given results from an individual pumping test, the spatial area over which properties are averaged must be considered. This area varies with strength of the test, aquifer properties, and other factors, so the true meaning of a contoured representation of parameter importance can be misleading.

The parameter-uncertainty analysis highlighted the importance that hydraulic conductivity has on the head prediction. Recharge also was found to be a large contributor to head-prediction uncertainty—although if recharge is already known reasonably well, the reduction in prediction uncertainty realized through better information about

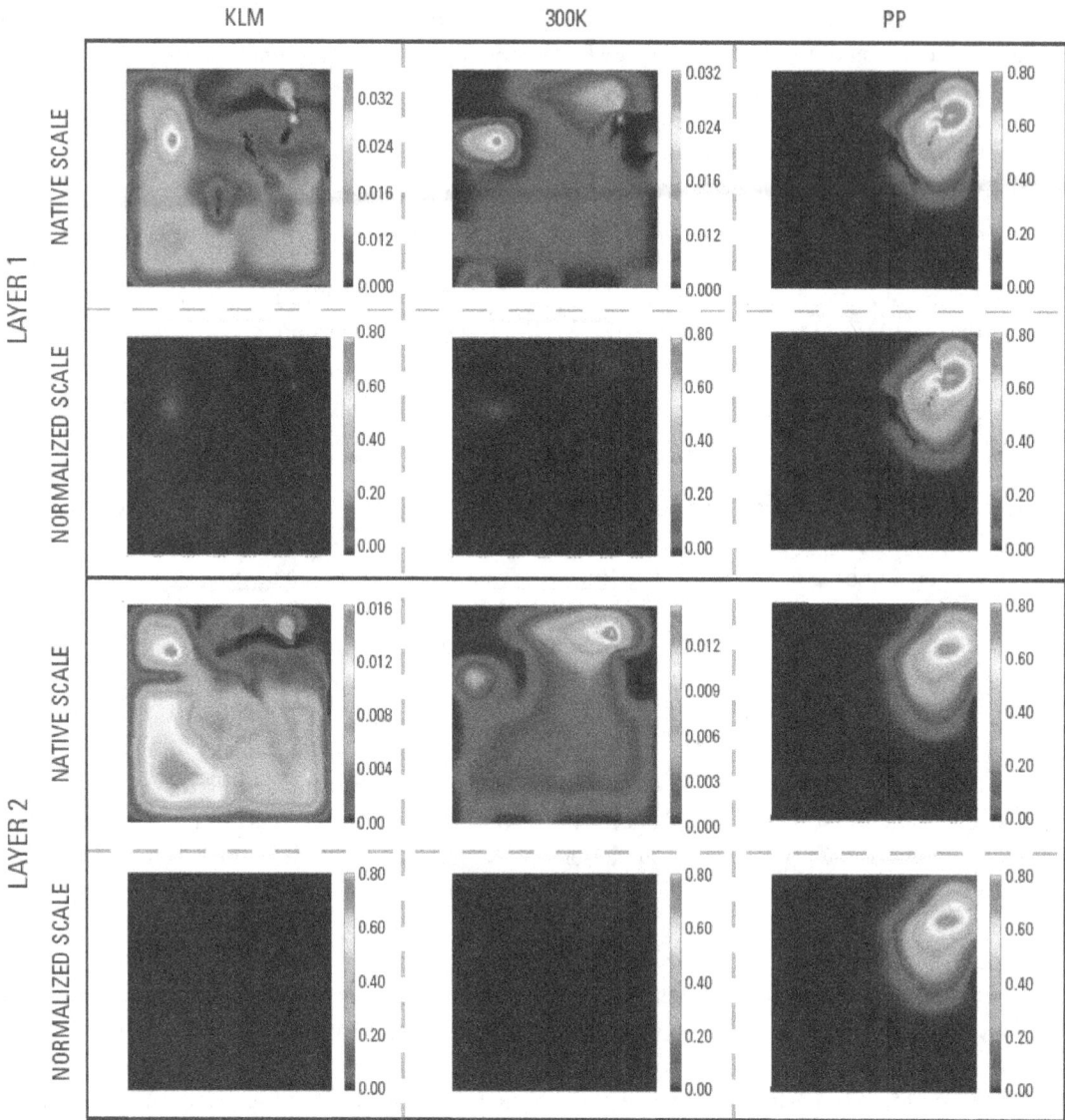

Figure 9. Observation data worth for flux-prediction scenario evaluated for layer 1 (upper 3 panels) and layer 2 (lower 3 panels). In each row of panels, three parameterizations are shown: KLM (left panel), 300K (middle panel) and PP (right panel). The values of data worth presented are normalized prediction uncertainty variance σ^2_{norm} calculated according to equation 5. Results are shown both at native scale to show detail and at a normalized scale relative to the PP results. The KLM, 300K, and PP parameterizations are described in the "Parameterization" section.

it will be limited. For the flux prediction, the largest contributor to prediction uncertainty was streambed conductance, an expected result because the streambed forms the connection between the surface-water and groundwater systems.

A network of potential head observations was then evaluated near both the location of a stress (pumping well) and two predictions (a head prediction near a stream, and the base flow in that

stream). The worth of each of the potential observations was calculated for each of the predictions, and the results were contoured. For a project manager deciding, with a limited budget, where to put a specified number of new wells in a monitoring network to calibrate the local model, this type of analysis could guide the design.

The worth of observations was calculated against a baseline condition of no available observations as the precalibration condition. The contoured data-worth results can guide network design in two ways. Using the results presented here, a manager could choose locations cascading down the data-worth scale from the most valuable to less valuable points in placing a predetermined number of wells. A more robust approach (but slightly more computationally costly) would be to progressively change the baseline with the addition of each proposed (and accepted) new well. This iterative procedure would change the location of the most valuable well each time the analysis was run contingent on the addition of each proposed new well. This is a Bayesian updating approach.

The number and arrangement of potential-head-observation locations used in this analysis is consistent with a thorough interrogation of the model domain. However, ranking the importance of this density of potential locations can be confounded by the level of parameterization used in the local model construction. In this example, the results are not meaningful for the KLM and 300K parameterization strategies. However, the PP parameterization with pilot points yields reasonable and intuitive results. This confounding influence of parameter oversimplification results from the increase in structural uncertainty (as a component of epistemic uncertainty). When a high level of parameter lumping is employed as a parameterization device, the calculation of uncertainty is overwhelmed by the errors introduced by oversimplification, and the difference to prediction uncertainty expected from the addition of a single potential observation is relegated to noise. Parameterization must be sufficiently fine that flexibility in the model diminishes the structural uncertainty so that the analysis of uncertainty desired for network design can be realized. This is in some ways an intuitive result; hydrologists have long known that oversimplification by analytical solutions or overly strict homogeneous, isotropic assumptions can result in poor representations of the response of natural systems. Yet, unless regularized inversion or other mathematical means are employed, the degree of additional complexity warranted is often left as a subjective decision for the modeler, uninvestigated in the context of uncertainty.

The results of the parameterization role in

uncertainty analysis, and the significant cost that can accompany simplifying the natural world into models, is consistent with the findings of Moore and Doherty (2006). It is important to note that the model objective (Hunt and Zheng, 1999; Hunt and others, 2007) again becomes critical for decision regarding the appropriate level of model complexity. Broad, piecewise-constant zones may represent prior knowledge about the hydrogeologic conceptualization of a model and may be appropriate for large-scale model predictions (see Haitjema, 1995, p. 272, 274, and 279); however, a model objective such as comparing the importance of one head observation in proximity to another potential location for a stream-aquifer prediction requires a parameterization scheme that may be finer than prior knowledge supports and one that is commensurate for the observation network being tested. Thus, use of models for monitoring-network design is likely to require a more flexible and highly parameterized approach to obtain meaningful results, even if the prediction itself can be simulated by using coarse parameter representations. That is, the parameterization should reflect the representative scale of the range of observations the model is to evaluate, not necessarily the scale of the original prediction of interest.

The final objective of this study was to investigate areas of theoretical equivalence for two freely available software packages that can perform network design and data-worth analysis. Prediction-uncertainty calculations by use of the equations of OPR-PPR and PREDUNC were found to be equivalent under a relatively narrow set of specific conditions and assumptions. PREDUNC (Doherty, 2008a,b) was chosen for the example analysis to explore a highly parameterized conceptualization in addition to sparsely parameterized conceptualizations. The current distribution of the OPR-PPR package (Tonkin and others, 2007) could not perform the full set of analyses because of limitations on the number of parameters that can be used when combining UCODE_2005 (Poeter and others, 2005) with OPR-PPR. In the final analysis, the differences in capabilities between OPR-PPR and PREDUNC are largely in the programming rather than the mathematics. However, in choosing a tool, the theoretical framework is a relevant factor and, as shown in this work and in the appendixes, the role of including *a priori* uncertainty and the explicit role of a Bayesian perspective are present in PREDUNC from derivation through application; in contrast, OPR-PPR is an adaptation of traditional, overdetermined regression. The goals of the project and the perspective of the user can be made to match one or the other perspective.

Acknowledgements

The authors thank Chris Hoard and Daniel Feinstein for providing their models for this work and for guidance regarding their use. Colleague reviews by Alyssa Dausman and Brian Clark improved the presentation of this work, as did an editorial review by Mike Eberle.

References

Banta, E.R., Poeter, E.P., Doherty, J.E., and Hill, M.C., 2006, JUPITER; Joint Universal Parameter IdenTification and Evaluation of Reliability—An application programming interface (API) for model analysis: U.S. Geological Survey Techniques and Methods, book 6, sec. E, chap. 1, 268 p.

Beven, Keith, 1993, Prophecy, reality and uncertainty in distributed hydrological modeling: Advances in Water Resources, v. 16, no. 1, p. 41–51

Beven, K.J., 2009, Environmental modelling; an uncertain future?—An introduction to techniques for uncertainty estimation in environmental prediction: London and New York, Routledge, 310 p.

Christensen, Steen, and Doherty, John, 2008, Predictive error dependencies when using pilot points and singular value decomposition in groundwater model calibration: Advances in Water Resources, v. 31, no 4, p. 674–700, doi:10.1016/j.advwatres.2008.01.003.

Cooley, R.L., 2004, A theory for modeling ground-water flow in heterogeneous media: U.S. Geological Survey Professional Paper 1679, 220 p.

Cooley, R.L., and Christensen, Steen, 2006, Bias and uncertainty in regression-calibrated models of groundwater flow in heterogeneous media: Advances in Water Resources, v. 29, no. 5, p. 639-656, doi:10.1016/j.advwatres.2005.07.012.

Cooley, R.L., and Naff, R.L., 1990, Regression modeling of ground-water flow: U.S. Geological Survey Techniques of Water-Resources Investigations, book 3, chap. B4, 232 p.

Dettinger, M.D., and Wilson, J.L., 1981, First-order analysis of uncertainty in numerical-models of groundwater-flow—Part 1. Mathematical development: Water Resources Research, v. 17, no. 1, p. 149-161.

Doherty, John, 2003, Ground water model calibration using pilot points and regularization: Ground Water, v. 41, no. 2, p. 170-177, doi:10.1111/j.1745-6584.2003.tb02580.x.

Doherty, John, 2008a, PEST, Model Independent Parameter Estimation—User manual (5th ed.): Brisbane, Australia, Watermark Numerical Computing (available at http://www.pesthomepage.org/.)

Doherty, John, 2008b, PEST, Model Independent Parameter Estimation—Addendum to User manual (5th ed.): Brisbane, Australia, Watermark Numerical Computing (available at http://www.pesthomepage.org/.)

Doherty, J.E., and Hunt, R.J., 2009, Two statistics for evaluating parameter identifiability and error reduction, Journal of Hydrology, v. 366, nos. 1–4, p. 119–127, doi:10.1016/j.jhydrol.2008.12.018.

Draper, N.R., and Smith, H., 1966, Applied regression analysis: New York, Wiley, 407 p.

Feinstein, D.T., Hunt, R.J., and Reeves, H.W., 2010, Regional groundwater-flow model of the Lake Michigan Basin in support of Great Lakes Basin water availability and use studies: U.S. Geological Survey Scientific Investigations Report 2010–5109, 379 p.

Fienen, M.N., Hunt, R.J., Krabbenhoft, D.P., and Clemo, Tom, 2009, Obtaining parsimonious hydraulic conductivity fields using head and transport observations—A Bayesian geostatistical parameter estimation approach: Water Resources Research, v. 45, no. 8, W08405, 23 p.

doi:10.1029/2008wr007431.

Fienen, M.N., Muffels, C.T., and Hunt, R.J., 2009, On constraining pilot point calibration with regularization in PEST: Ground Water, v. 47, no. 6, p. 835–844, doi:10.1111/j.1745-6584.2009.00579.x.

Glasgow, H.S., Fortney, M.D., Lee, J.J., Graettinger, A.J., and Reeves, H.W., 2003, MODFLOW 2000 head uncertainty, a first-order second moment method: Ground Water, v. 41, no. 3, p. 342–350.

Haitjema, H.M., 1995, Analytic element modeling of groundwater flow: San Diego, Academic Press, 394 p.

Harbaugh, A. W., 2005, MODFLOW-2005, the U.S. Geological Survey modular ground-water model—the Ground-Water Flow Process: U.S. Geological Survey Techniques and Methods, book 6, chap. A–16, 256 p.

Hoard, C.J., 2010, Implementation of local grid refinement in MODFLOW for the Lake Michigan Basin regional groundwater flow model: U.S. Geological Survey Scientific Investigations Report 2010–5117, 25 p.

Hunt, Randy, and Zheng, Chunmiao, 1999, Debating complexity in modeling: Eos, Transactions, American Geophysical Union, v. 80, no. 3, p. 29.

Hunt, R. J., 2002, Evaluating the importance of future data collection sites using parameter estimation and analytic element groundwater flow models, *in* International Conference on Computational Methods in Water Resources Conference, Fourteenth, Delft, The Netherlands: Elsevier, v. 1, p. 755–762.

Hunt, R.J., Doherty, John, and Tonkin, M.J., 2007, Are models too simple? Arguments for increased parameterization: Ground Water, v. 45, no. 3, p. 254–262, doi:10.1111/j.1745-6584.2007.00316.x.

Kunstmann, Harald, Kinzelbach, Wolfgang, and Siegfried, Tobias, 2002, Conditional first-order second-moment method and its application to the quantification of uncertainty in groundwater modeling: Water Resources Research, v. 38, no. 4, 14 p., doi:10.1029/2000wr000022

Mehl, S.W., and Hill, M.C., 2005, MODFLOW-2005, the U.S. Geological Survey modular groundwater model:—Documentation of shared node local grid refinement (LGR) and the boundary flow and head (BFH) package: U.S. Geological Survey Techniques and Methods 6–A12, 68 p.

Moore, Catherine, and Doherty, John, 2005, Role of the calibration process in reducing model predictive error: Water Resources Research, v. 41, no. 5, W05020 14 p., doi:10.1029/2004WR003501.

Moore, Catherine, and Doherty, John, 2006, The cost of uniqueness in groundwater model calibration: Advances in Water Resources, v. 29, no. 4, p. 605–623, doi:10.1016/j.advwatres.2005.07.003.

Poeter, E.P., Hill, M.C., Banta, E.R., Mehl, Steffen, and Christensen, Steen, 2005, UCODE_2005 and six other computer codes for universal sensitivity analysis, calibration, and uncertainty—Evaluation version 1.015, Tech. rep., U. S. Geological Survey Techniques and Methods 6–A11, 283 p.

Rubin, Y., 2003, Applied stochastic hydrogeology: Oxford and New York, Oxford University Press, 391 p.

Tonkin, M.J., Tiedeman, C.R., Ely, M.D., and Hill, M.C., 2007, OPR-PPR, a computer program for assessing data importance to model predictions using linear statistics: U.S. Geological Survey Techniques and Methods 6E2, 115 p.

Tonkin, M.J., Tiedeman, C.R., Ely, M.D., and Hill, M.C., 2008, Errata for OPR-PPR, a computer program for assessing data importance to model predictions using linear statistics: Addendum to U.S. Geological Survey Techniques and Methods 6—E2, 1 p., accessed February 4, 2010, at *http://pubs.usgs.gov/tm/2007/tm6e2/pdf/tm_6-e2-errata.pdf.*

Appendix 1—Derivation of PREDUNC equations in a Bayesian Context

This appendix presents a derivation of the PREDUNC statistic calculated in equation 1 for the variance of a prediction. The derivation here is based on Bayesian conditioning and is preceded by preliminaries for readers less familiar with the mathematics used here. The derivations are based largely on discussion by Anderson (1984) and Olaf Cirpka (Subsurface Mixing And Reactive Transport (SMART) workgroup, Universität Stuttgart, Institut für Wasserbau, written commun., 2003)

Preliminaries

For a general random variable that is multi-Gaussian, the equation for its distribution is

$$p\left(\mathbf{x}\right) = \frac{1}{\sqrt{(2\pi)^n |\mathbf{C_{11}}|}} \exp\left(-\frac{1}{2}\left(\mathbf{x_1} - \mu_{\mathbf{x_1}}\right)^T \mathbf{C_{11}^{-1}}\left(\mathbf{x_1} - \mu_{\mathbf{x_1}}\right)\right) \tag{1.1}$$

where $\mathbf{x_1}$ is the random variable, $\mu_{\mathbf{x_1}}$ is its mean, and $\mathbf{C_{11}}$ is its covariance. The convention is that for dummy variables such as $\mathbf{x_1}$ and $\mathbf{x_2}$, $\mu_{\mathbf{x_1}}$ is the mean of $\mathbf{x_1}$, $\mu_{\mathbf{x_2}}$ is mean of $\mathbf{x_2}$, $\mathbf{C_{11}}$ is the covariance of $\mathbf{x_1}$, $\mathbf{C_{22}}$ is the covariance of $\mathbf{x_2}$, and $\mathbf{C_{12}}$ is the cross-covariance of $\mathbf{x_1}$ and $\mathbf{x_2}$. The cross-covariance is symmetric, so $\mathbf{C_{12}} = \mathbf{C_{21}}$. All lowercase bold values indicate vectors, whereas capital bold letters indicate matrices. Such a multi-Gaussian (also called normal) distribution can be noted in shorthand as $\mathbf{x_1} \sim N\left(\mu_{\mathbf{x_1}}, \mathbf{C_{11}}\right)$ which implies the equation above.

The definition of covariance is

$$\mathbf{C_{12}} = E\left[\left(\mathbf{x_1} - \mu_{\mathbf{x_1}}\right)\left(\mathbf{x_2} - \mu_{\mathbf{x_2}}\right)^T\right] \tag{1.2}$$

where $E\left[\,\right]$ is the expected value.

The next preliminary element is a definition of conditioning. If we start with two multi-Gaussian random variables $\mathbf{x_1}$ and $\mathbf{x_2}$ with means $\mu_{\mathbf{x_1}}$ and $\mu_{\mathbf{x_2}}$ and covariance matrices $\mathbf{C_{11}}$ and $\mathbf{C_{22}}$, we can condition $\mathbf{x_2}$ on $\mathbf{x_1} = \mathbf{x_1^{(0)}}$, leading to the two following key relationships:

$$\tilde{\mu}_{\mathbf{x_2}} = \mu_{\mathbf{x_2}} + \mathbf{C_{21}}\mathbf{C_{11}^{-1}}\left(\mathbf{x_1^{(0)}} - \mu_{\mathbf{x_1}}\right) \tag{1.3}$$

$$\tilde{\mathbf{C}}_{\mathbf{22}} = \mathbf{C_{22}} - \mathbf{C_{21}}\mathbf{C_{11}^{-1}}\mathbf{C_{12}} \tag{1.4}$$

where $\tilde{\mu}_{\mathbf{x_2}}$ is the conditional mean of $\mathbf{x_2}$ and $\tilde{\mathbf{C}}_{\mathbf{22}}$ is the conditional covariance of the dependent variable $\mathbf{x_2}$. Note that, in this case, $\mathbf{x_1}$ is the independent variable, and $\mathbf{x_2}$—the dependent variable—is being conditioned upon $\mathbf{x_1}$. The value $\mathbf{x_1^{(0)}}$ is some realization or measurement from the distribution of $\mathbf{x_1}$. In the parameter-estimation case below, for the problem of inference, $\mathbf{x_1}$ would correspond to the observations ($\mathbf{h}$) and $\mathbf{x_2}$ would correspond to the parameters ($\mathbf{p}$). As a result, the conditioning occurs when we have specific measurements in $\mathbf{h}$ upon which to base the parameter estimates.

Conditioning Without Epistemic Error

Assume we have two random variables $\mathbf{p}$ and $\mathbf{h}$, which are both multi-Gaussian. Further assume $\mathbf{p}$ corresponds to model parameters with mean $\mu_{\mathbf{p}}$ and covariance $\mathbf{C_{pp}}$ and $\mathbf{h}$ corresponds to model outputs with mean $\mu_{\mathbf{h}}$ and covariance matrix $\mathbf{C_{hh}}$. We assume a linear relationship between $\mathbf{h}$ and $\mathbf{p}$ that is expressed through the measurement equation as

$$\mathbf{h} = \mathbf{Xp} \tag{1.5}$$

In nonlinear cases, $\mathbf{X}$ is the sensitivity matrix (Jacobian) defined as $\mathbf{X} = \frac{\partial \mathbf{h}}{\partial \mathbf{p}}$. For linear theory, however, $\mathbf{X}$ just has to be some linear relationship.

Now, suppose we want to express the linear change in $\mu_\mathbf{p}$ conditioned on the knowledge of a new set of measurements $\mathbf{h_0}$. This is the opposite direction that this derivation would normally follow because it is a problem of inference. First, we consider the conditional mean ($\tilde{\mu}_\mathbf{p}$), which will become

$$\tilde{\mu}_\mathbf{p} = \mu_\mathbf{p} + \mathbf{B}\left(\mathbf{h_0} - \mu_\mathbf{h}\right) \tag{1.6}$$

Next, we calculate the conditional covariance of $\mathbf{p}$, defined as $\tilde{\mathbf{C}}_\mathbf{pp}$, using the definition of cross-covariance in equation 1.2,

$$
\begin{aligned}
\tilde{\mathbf{C}}_\mathbf{pp} &= E\left[(\mathbf{p} - \tilde{\mu}_\mathbf{p})(\mathbf{p} - \tilde{\mu}_\mathbf{p})^T\right] \\
&= E\left[\{(\mathbf{p} - \mu_\mathbf{p}) - (\mathbf{B}(\mathbf{h_0} - \mu_\mathbf{h}))\}\{(\mathbf{p} - \mu_\mathbf{p}) - (\mathbf{B}(\mathbf{h_0} - \mu_\mathbf{h}))\}^T\right] \\
&= E\left[(\mathbf{p} - \mu_\mathbf{p}) - (\mathbf{p} - \mu_\mathbf{p})^T - 2\mathbf{B}(\mathbf{h_0} - \mu_\mathbf{h})(\mathbf{p} - \mu_\mathbf{p})^T + \mathbf{B}(\mathbf{h_0} - \mu_\mathbf{h})(\mathbf{h_0} - \mu_\mathbf{h})^T \mathbf{B}^T\right] \\
&= E\left[(\mathbf{p} - \mu_\mathbf{p}) - (\mathbf{p} - \mu_\mathbf{p})^T\right] - 2\mathbf{B}E\left[(\mathbf{h_0} - \mu_\mathbf{h})(\mathbf{p} - \mu_\mathbf{p})^T\right] \\
&\quad + \mathbf{B}E\left[(\mathbf{h_0} - \mu_\mathbf{h})(\mathbf{h_0} - \mu_\mathbf{h})^T \mathbf{B}^T\right] \\
&= \mathbf{C}_\mathbf{pp} - 2\mathbf{B}\mathbf{C}_\mathbf{hp} + \mathbf{B}\mathbf{C}_\mathbf{hh}\mathbf{B}^T \tag{1.7}
\end{aligned}
$$

Now, we need to find correct values of $\mathbf{B}$. We seek the most likely mean, which corresponds with the minimum variance value. So, we seek $\mathbf{B}$ that minimizes $\tilde{\mathbf{C}}_\mathbf{pp}$. This is accomplished by setting the derivative of $\tilde{\mathbf{C}}_\mathbf{pp}$ (from equation 1.7) with respect to $\mathbf{B}$ to zero:

$$
\begin{aligned}
\frac{\partial \tilde{\mathbf{C}}_\mathbf{pp}}{\partial \mathbf{B}} &= \mathbf{0} \\
-2\mathbf{C}_\mathbf{hp} + 2\mathbf{C}_\mathbf{hh}\mathbf{B}^T &= \mathbf{0} \\
\mathbf{C}_\mathbf{hh}\mathbf{B}^T &= \mathbf{C}_\mathbf{hp} \\
\mathbf{B}\mathbf{C}_\mathbf{hh} &= \mathbf{C}_\mathbf{ph} \\
\mathbf{B} &= \mathbf{C}_\mathbf{ph}\mathbf{C}_\mathbf{hh}^{-1} \tag{1.8}
\end{aligned}
$$

Substituting our new-found value of $\mathbf{B}$ back into equation 1.6, we see that the conditional mean is mapped from the unconditional mean using the covariances

$$\tilde{\mu}_\mathbf{p} = \mu_\mathbf{p} + \mathbf{C}_\mathbf{ph}\mathbf{C}_\mathbf{hh}^{-1}\left(\mathbf{h_0} - \mu_\mathbf{h}\right) \tag{1.9}$$

To find the new conditional covariance on the parameters $\tilde{\mathbf{C}}_\mathbf{pp}$, we substitute $\mathbf{B}$ into equation 1.7, and noting that because $\mathbf{C}_\mathbf{hh}$ is a symmetric matrix by definition, $\left(\mathbf{C}_\mathbf{hh}^{-1}\right)^T = \mathbf{C}_\mathbf{hh}^{-1}$

$$
\begin{aligned}
\tilde{\mathbf{C}}_\mathbf{pp} &= \mathbf{C}_\mathbf{pp} - 2\mathbf{B}\mathbf{C}_\mathbf{ph} + \mathbf{B}\mathbf{C}_\mathbf{hh}\mathbf{B}^T \\
&= \mathbf{C}_\mathbf{pp} - 2\mathbf{C}_\mathbf{ph}\mathbf{C}_\mathbf{hh}^{-1}\mathbf{C}_\mathbf{hp} + \mathbf{C}_\mathbf{ph}\mathbf{C}_\mathbf{hh}^{-1}\mathbf{C}_\mathbf{hh}\left(\mathbf{C}_\mathbf{hh}^{-1}\right)^T \mathbf{C}_\mathbf{hp} \\
&= \mathbf{C}_\mathbf{pp} - \mathbf{C}_\mathbf{ph}\mathbf{C}_\mathbf{hh}^{-1}\mathbf{C}_\mathbf{hp} \tag{1.10}
\end{aligned}
$$

This is consistent with the given propagation formula of equation 1.4. What we have established here is that, starting with two multi-Gaussian distributions, we can condition one upon the other—which is the same as converting $\mathbf{p} \sim N(\mu_\mathbf{p}, \mathbf{C}_\mathbf{pp})$ into $\mathbf{p}|\mathbf{h} \sim N(\tilde{\mu}_\mathbf{p}, \tilde{\mathbf{C}}_\mathbf{pp})$, which is the conditional random variable. In the next section, we extend this to the case where the conditioning occurs in the presence of epistemic error, and then we move on to the Bayesian interpretation.

Conditioning With Epistemic Error

Now we revise the measurement equation of equation 1.5 by corrupting the observations $\mathbf{h}$ with normally distributed epistemic error ε with zero mean and covariance matrix $\mathbf{C}_{\varepsilon\varepsilon}$

$$\mathbf{h} = \mathbf{Xp} + \varepsilon \tag{1.11}$$

Rather than repeat the entire procedure of the previous section using equation 1.11, we can simply replace $\mathbf{C}_{\mathbf{hh}}^{-1}$ in equation 1.10. To derive a new version of $\mathbf{C}_{\mathbf{hh}}^{-1}$, we return to the definition of covariance in equation 1.2:

$$\mathbf{C}_{\mathbf{hh}} = E\left[(\mathbf{h} - \mu_{\mathbf{h}})(\mathbf{h} - \mu_{\mathbf{h}})^T\right] \tag{1.12}$$

We can replace $\mathbf{h}$ with equation 1.11, recalling that $\mu_{\mathbf{x}} = E[\mathbf{x}]$ and expectation is distributive, and do some algebra as follows

$$\mathbf{C}_{\mathbf{hh}} = E\left[(\mathbf{Xp} + \varepsilon - E[\mathbf{Xp} + \varepsilon])(\mathbf{Xp} + \varepsilon - E[\mathbf{Xp} + \varepsilon])^T\right] \tag{1.13}$$

$$= E\left[(\mathbf{Xp} + \varepsilon - \mathbf{X}E[\mathbf{p}] - E[\varepsilon])(\mathbf{Xp} + \varepsilon - \mathbf{X}E[\mathbf{p}] - E[\varepsilon])^T\right] \tag{1.14}$$

Recall that we assumed ε has mean zero, so we can drop the $E[\varepsilon]$ terms and rearrange

$$= E\left[(\mathbf{X}(\mathbf{p} - E[\mathbf{p}]) + \varepsilon)(\mathbf{X}(\mathbf{p} - E[\mathbf{p}]) + \varepsilon)^T\right] \tag{1.15}$$

$$= E\left[(\mathbf{X}(\mathbf{p} - E[\mathbf{p}]))(\mathbf{X}(\mathbf{p} - E[\mathbf{p}]))^T\right] + E\left[(\mathbf{X}(\mathbf{p} - E[\mathbf{p}]))\varepsilon^T\right] + E\left[\varepsilon\varepsilon^T\right] \tag{1.16}$$

Now, looking at the first term,

$$E\left[(\mathbf{X}(\mathbf{p} - E[\mathbf{p}]))(\mathbf{X}(\mathbf{p} - E[\mathbf{p}]))^T\right] \tag{1.17}$$

$$= E\left[(\mathbf{X}(\mathbf{p} - E[\mathbf{p}]))(\mathbf{p} - E[\mathbf{p}])^T\mathbf{X}^T\right] \tag{1.18}$$

$$= \mathbf{X}E\left[(\mathbf{p} - E[\mathbf{p}])(\mathbf{p} - E[\mathbf{p}])^T\right]\mathbf{X}^T \tag{1.19}$$

$$= \mathbf{X}\mathbf{C}_{\mathbf{pp}}\mathbf{X}^T \tag{1.20}$$

using equation 1.2 to define $\mathbf{C}_{\mathbf{pp}}$.
Now, on to the second term,

$$E\left[(\mathbf{X}(\mathbf{p} - E[\mathbf{p}]))\varepsilon^T\right] \tag{1.21}$$

$$= E\left[\mathbf{Xp}\varepsilon^T\right] - E\left[\mathbf{X}E[\mathbf{p}]\varepsilon^T\right] = 0 \tag{1.22}$$

recalling that $E[E[\mathbf{p}]] = \mathbf{p}$
Finally, we tackle the third term, using the definitions of ε at the beginning of this section, including the mean being equal to zero:

$$E\left[\mathbf{vv}^T\right] = E\left[(\mathbf{v} - 0)(\mathbf{v} - 0)^T\right] = \mathbf{C}_{\varepsilon\varepsilon} \tag{1.23}$$

Reassembling the first and third terms,

$$\mathbf{C_{hh}} = \mathbf{X}\mathbf{C_{pp}}\mathbf{X}^T + \mathbf{C}_{\varepsilon\varepsilon} \tag{1.24}$$

Substituting back into equation 1.10,

$$\tilde{\mathbf{C}}_{pp} = \mathbf{C_{pp}} - \mathbf{C_{ph}}\left[\mathbf{X}\mathbf{C_{pp}}\mathbf{X}^T + \mathbf{C}_{\varepsilon\varepsilon}\right]^{-1}\mathbf{C_{hp}} \tag{1.25}$$

Now, we need to define $\mathbf{C_{hp}}$ by using equation 1.2:

$$
\begin{aligned}
\mathbf{C_{hp}} &= E\left[\left(\mathbf{X}\mathbf{p} + \varepsilon - E\left[\mathbf{X}\mathbf{p} + \varepsilon\right]\right)\left(\mathbf{p} - E\left[\mathbf{p}\right]\right)^T\right] & (1.26)\\
&= E\left[\left(\mathbf{X}\mathbf{p} + \varepsilon - \mathbf{X}E\left[\mathbf{p}\right]\right)\left(\mathbf{p} - E\left[\mathbf{p}\right]\right)^T\right] & (1.27)\\
&= E\left[\mathbf{X}\left(\mathbf{p} - E\left[\mathbf{p}\right]\right)\left(\mathbf{p} - E\left[\mathbf{p}\right]\right)^T + \varepsilon\left(\mathbf{p} - E\left[\mathbf{p}\right]\right)\right] & (1.28)\\
&= \mathbf{X}E\left[\left(\mathbf{p} - E\left[\mathbf{p}\right]\right)\left(\mathbf{p} - E\left[\mathbf{p}\right]\right)^T\right] + E\left[\varepsilon\mathbf{p}^T\right] - E\left[\varepsilon E[\mathbf{p}]^T\right] & (1.29)\\
&= \mathbf{X}\mathbf{C_{pp}} & (1.30)
\end{aligned}
$$

Then,

$$\tilde{\mathbf{C}}_{pp} = \mathbf{C_{pp}} - \mathbf{C_{pp}}\mathbf{X}^T\left[\mathbf{X}\mathbf{C_{pp}}\mathbf{X}^T + \mathbf{C}_{\varepsilon\varepsilon}\right]^{-1}\mathbf{X}\mathbf{C_{pp}} \tag{1.31}$$

resulting in the new conditional covariance on the parameters.

A Bayesian Interpretation

We start with Bayes' theorem

$$p\left(\mathbf{p}|\mathbf{h}\right) = \frac{p\left(\mathbf{h}|\mathbf{p}\right)p\left(\mathbf{p}\right)}{p\left(\mathbf{h}\right)} \tag{1.32}$$

We define $p\left(\mathbf{p}|\mathbf{h}\right)$ as the posterior probability or the probability of the parameters given (conditional on) the data; $p\left(\mathbf{h}|\mathbf{p}\right)$ as the likelihood function, meaning how likely is it that we perfectly reproduce our observations (which correspond to $\mathbf{h}$) given the parameters $\mathbf{p}$; $p\left(\mathbf{p}\right)$ as the prior probability of the parameters; and $p\left(\mathbf{h}\right)$ as the total probability of $\mathbf{h}$. $p\left(\mathbf{h}\right)$ is really the probability of all possible data realizations integrated across parameter space. This is often difficult to calculate and is constant with respect to this problem; so, to within a constant, we can restate the theorem to

$$p\left(\mathbf{p}|\mathbf{h}\right) \propto p\left(\mathbf{h}|\mathbf{p}\right)p\left(\mathbf{p}\right) \tag{1.33}$$

If we seek a maximum likelihood solution (which requires all these distributions to be multi-Gaussian), then the constant of proportionality will not alter the conclusion of which set of parameters ($\mathbf{p}$) maximizes the posterior probability $p\left(\mathbf{p}|\mathbf{h}\right)$.

An Important Caveat

If we have fully defined probability density functions, then we have values for the means $\mu_\mathbf{p}$ and $\mu_\mathbf{h}$. In reality, our knowledge of these means is diffuse, so the results of this section are a simplification and more rigor must be used to find the answer. However, we proceed assuming we know the means.

To find $p(\mathbf{p}|\mathbf{h})$ becomes a matter of conditioning as shown above. In general terms, this can be shown with partitioned matrices. We define

$$p(\mathbf{h}|\mathbf{p}) \sim N\left(\mu_\mathbf{h}, \mathbf{C_{hh}} = \mathbf{XC_{pp}X^T} + \mathbf{C}_{\varepsilon\varepsilon}\right) \tag{1.34}$$

$$p(\mathbf{p}) \sim N(\mu_\mathbf{p}, \mathbf{C_{pp}}) \tag{1.35}$$

Now we express the conditioning as

$$\begin{bmatrix} \mathbf{h}|\mathbf{p} \\ \mathbf{p} \end{bmatrix} = \begin{bmatrix} \mathbf{I} & \mathbf{X} \\ \mathbf{0} & \mathbf{I} \end{bmatrix} \begin{bmatrix} \varepsilon \\ \mathbf{p} \end{bmatrix} \tag{1.36}$$

the conditional relationship of $\mathbf{h}$ on $\mathbf{p}$ shown as $\mathbf{h}|\mathbf{p}$ above is assumed from here on without explicitly being notated.

Using the formula for the propagation of variance

$$cov\left(\begin{bmatrix} \mathbf{h} \\ \mathbf{p} \end{bmatrix}\right) = \begin{bmatrix} \mathbf{I} & \mathbf{X} \\ \mathbf{0} & \mathbf{I} \end{bmatrix} \begin{bmatrix} \mathbf{C}_{hh} & \mathbf{0} \\ \mathbf{0} & \mathbf{C}_{pp} \end{bmatrix} \begin{bmatrix} \mathbf{I} & \mathbf{0} \\ \mathbf{X}^T & \mathbf{I} \end{bmatrix} \tag{1.37}$$

$$= \begin{bmatrix} \mathbf{X}_{obs}\mathbf{C}_{pp}\mathbf{X}_{obs}^T + \mathbf{C}_{\varepsilon\varepsilon} & \mathbf{XC}_{pp} \\ \mathbf{C}_{pp}\mathbf{X}^T & \mathbf{C}_{pp} \end{bmatrix} \tag{1.38}$$

Now, we return to the general form of equation 1.4 but remembering that, in the inverse problem, $\mathbf{p}$ is dependent (conditioned) on $\mathbf{h}$:

$$cov\left(\begin{bmatrix} \mathbf{x}_1 \\ \mathbf{x}_2 \end{bmatrix}\right) = \begin{bmatrix} \mathbf{C}_{11} & \mathbf{C}_{12} \\ \mathbf{C}_{21} & \mathbf{C}_{22} \end{bmatrix} \tag{1.39}$$

$$\tilde{\mathbf{C}}_{22} = \mathbf{C}_{22} - \mathbf{C}_{21}\mathbf{C}_{11}^{-1}\mathbf{C}_{12} \tag{1.40}$$

So,

$$\tilde{\mathbf{C}}_{pp} = \mathbf{C}_{pp} - \mathbf{C}_{pp}\mathbf{X}^T\left[\mathbf{XC}_{pp}\mathbf{X}^T + \mathbf{C}_{\varepsilon\varepsilon}\right]^{-1}\mathbf{XC}_{pp} \tag{1.41}$$

which is the same result as found in equation 1.31.

Making a Prediction

Up until now, we have been concerned with the propagation of covariance, due to application of Bayes' theorem, from a set of measurements $\mathbf{h}$ to the inferred set of parameters $\mathbf{p}$. We can take this propagation one step further if we have a linear transformation of the parameters such as

$$s = \mathbf{y}^T\mathbf{p} \tag{1.42}$$

where $\mathbf{y}$ is a vector representing a linear transformation to prediction (s) made on the basis of a set of parameters $\mathbf{p}$.

Now, we have already propagated the covariance from $\mathbf{h}$ to $\mathbf{p}$ through Bayes' theorem for inference. We can incorporate this other linear transformation to yield the variance of the scalar precision (s). We just need to set up our matrix so that we are conditioning s on $\mathbf{h}$:

$$\begin{bmatrix} \mathbf{h}|\mathbf{p} \\ s \end{bmatrix} = \begin{bmatrix} \mathbf{I} & \mathbf{X} \\ 0 & \mathbf{y}^T \end{bmatrix} \begin{bmatrix} \varepsilon \\ \mathbf{p} \end{bmatrix} \tag{1.43}$$

Again, the explicit conditionality of $\mathbf{h}$ on $\mathbf{p}$ is dropped for clarity.

Then,

$$\begin{aligned} cov\left(\begin{bmatrix} \mathbf{h} \\ s \end{bmatrix}\right) &= \begin{bmatrix} \mathbf{I} & \mathbf{X} \\ \mathbf{0} & \mathbf{y}^T \end{bmatrix} \begin{bmatrix} \mathbf{C}_{hh} & \mathbf{0} \\ \mathbf{0} & \mathbf{C}_{pp} \end{bmatrix} \begin{bmatrix} \mathbf{I} & \mathbf{0} \\ \mathbf{X}^T & \mathbf{y} \end{bmatrix} \\ &= \begin{bmatrix} \mathbf{X}_{obs}\mathbf{C}_{pp}\mathbf{X}_{obs}^T + \mathbf{C}_{\varepsilon\varepsilon} & \mathbf{X}\mathbf{C}_{pp}\mathbf{y} \\ \mathbf{y}^T\mathbf{C}_{pp}\mathbf{X}^T & \mathbf{y}^T\mathbf{C}_{pp}\mathbf{y} \end{bmatrix} \end{aligned} \tag{1.44}$$

And finally, again applying equation 1.4, we find

$$\sigma_s^2 = \mathbf{y}^T\mathbf{C}_{pp}\mathbf{y} - \mathbf{y}^T\mathbf{C}_{pp}\mathbf{X}^T\left[\mathbf{X}_{obs}\mathbf{C}_{pp}\mathbf{X}_{obs}^T + \mathbf{C}_{\varepsilon\varepsilon}\right]^{-1}\mathbf{X}\mathbf{C}_{pp}\mathbf{y} \tag{1.45}$$

This is the same equation as 4.37 in Doherty (2008b), recalling that s is a scalar prediction, so σ_s^2 is a single variance value rather than a covariance matrix.

References

Anderson, T.W., 1984, An introduction to multivariate statistical analysis (2d ed.): New York, Wiley, Wiley series in probability and mathematical statistics, 675 p.

Doherty, John, 2008b, PEST, Model Independent Parameter Estimation—Addendum to User manual (5th ed.): Brisbane, Australia, Watermark Numerical Computing (available at http://www.pesthomepage.org/.)

Appendix 2—Derivation of OPR-PPR Statistics

The OPR-PPR statistics are based on an assumption of overdetermined weighted least-squares regression. To obtain the equation for posterior prediction uncertainty in equation 1 in Tonkin and others (2007, p. 5) we first must determine a value for $\mathbf{V}$ through equation 2 in Tonkin and others (2007, p. 5),

$$\mathbf{V} = s^2 \left(\mathbf{X}^T \mathbf{C}_{\varepsilon\varepsilon}^{-1} \mathbf{X} \right)^{-1} \tag{2.1}$$

where $\mathbf{V}$ is the parameter variance-covariance matrix found through overdetermined weighted least squares regression and $\mathbf{C}_{\varepsilon\varepsilon}^{-1}$ corresponds to ω in Tonkin and others (2007, p. 5), and s^2 is the calculated error variance from the model calibration (Tonkin and others, 2007, p. 6). In the underdetermined case, where $NPAR > NOBS$, equation 2.1 must be supplemented with prior information, in which case $\mathbf{X}$ is appended to.

To account for a prediction, we define $\mathbf{s} = \mathbf{Z}\mathbf{p}$, where $\mathbf{Z}$ is the sensitivity of the predictions to the parameters and, using the definition of covariance,

$$\begin{aligned}
\mathbf{C}_{ss} &= E\left[(\mathbf{s} - E[\mathbf{s}])(\mathbf{s} - E[\mathbf{s}])^T \right] \\
&= E\left[(\mathbf{Z}\mathbf{p} - E[\mathbf{Z}\mathbf{p}])(\mathbf{Z}\mathbf{p} - E[\mathbf{Z}\mathbf{p}])^T \right] \\
&= E\left[(\mathbf{Z}(\mathbf{p} - E[\mathbf{p}]))(\mathbf{Z}(\mathbf{p} - E[\mathbf{p}]))^T \right] \\
&= \mathbf{Z}E\left[(\mathbf{p} - E[\mathbf{p}])(\mathbf{p} - E[\mathbf{p}])^T \right]\mathbf{Z}^T \\
&= \mathbf{Z}\mathbf{C}_{pp}\mathbf{Z}^T
\end{aligned} \tag{2.2}$$

$\mathbf{V}$ in equation 2.1 is equivalent to $\mathbf{C}_{pp}$ in equation 2.2. $\mathbf{V}$ by equation 2.1 is typically calculated as the covariance of the estimated parameters following an overdetermined least-squares regression (Draper and Smith, 1966, p. 80; Cooley and Naff, 1990, p. 167). Replacing $\mathbf{Z}$ with $\mathbf{y}^T$, signifying that we are interested only in a single prediction such that $\mathbf{y}^T$ is a row from $\mathbf{Z}$, we obtain

$$\sigma_s^2 = s^2 \mathbf{y}^T \left(\mathbf{X}^T \mathbf{C}_{\varepsilon\varepsilon}^{-1} \mathbf{X} \right)^{-1} \mathbf{y} \tag{2.3}$$

This equation is equivalent to equation 1 in Tonkin and others (2007, p. 5), although the symbology is different to facilitate comparison with other equations in this report.

References

Cooley, R.L., and Naff, R.L., 1990, Regression modeling of ground-water flow: U.S. Geological Survey Techniques of Water-Resources Investigations, book 3, chap. B4, 232 p.

Draper, N.R., and Smith, H., 1966, Applied regression analysis: New York, Wiley, 407 p.

Tonkin, M.J., Tiedeman, C.R., Ely, M.D., and Hill, M.C., 2007, OPR-PPR, a computer program for assessing data importance to model predictions using linear statistics: U.S. Geological Survey Techniques and Methods 6E2, 115 p.

Appendix 3—Conditions Under Which OPR-PPR and PREDUNC Give the Same Results

Doherty and Hunt (2009) suggest that, based on the theory outlined in appendix 2, it is possible for OPR-PPR using equation 2.3 and PREDUNC using equation 1 to give the same results for a restrictive set of conditions. For this to occur, two additional parameters and five assumptions must be specified. These are encapsulated by the process described below.

In terms of parameters, we must partition the Jacobian matrix $\mathbf{X}$,

$$\mathbf{X} = \begin{bmatrix} \mathbf{X}_{obs} \\ \mathbf{X}_{pri} \end{bmatrix} \tag{3.1}$$

where $\mathbf{X}_{obs}$ is the sensitivity of observations to parameters and $\mathbf{X}_{pri}$ is the sensitivity of prior information to parameters. Also, we must concatenate the two covariance matrices from equation 1 into a single matrix $(\mathbf{C})$ that replaces $\mathbf{C}_{\varepsilon\varepsilon}^{-1}$ in equation 2.3,

$$\mathbf{C} = \begin{bmatrix} \mathbf{C}_{\varepsilon\varepsilon}^{-1} & \mathbf{0} \\ \mathbf{0} & \mathbf{C}_{pp}^{-1} \end{bmatrix} \tag{3.2}$$

noting that these matrices are the inverse of the covariance of epistemic uncertainty and parameter variability, respectively.

The use of prior information in this way is necessary to incorporate information regarding the inherent variability of the parameters into the problem (that is, the $\mathbf{C}_{pp}$ matrix of equation 1). The regularization equations do not enter the calculations of equation 1, even if regularization is used with PREDUNC (such as commonly done in the case of a pilot-points implementation).

The value for s^2 in equation 2.3 is defined in Hill and Tiedeman (2007, p. 95) as

$$s^2 = \frac{S(\mathbf{p})}{NOBS + NPRIOR - NPAR} \tag{3.3}$$

where $S(\mathbf{p})$ is the weighted sum of squares residuals using $\mathbf{C}^{-1}$ as the matrix of weights. In an idealized postcalibration condition, the value of s^2 should approach unity.

Given this development of the problem, the following conditions must now be met for OPR-PPR and PREDUNC to yield the same results:

1. The value of s^2 in equation 2.3 must be equal to unity.

2. The prior information must be of the form $\mathbf{p} = \mathbf{p}_{pri}$, where $\mathbf{p}_{pri}$ is an *a priori* set of preferred values for the parameters $\mathbf{p}$. This is done so that $\mathbf{X}_{pri} = \frac{\partial p_{pri_i}}{\partial p_j}$ is an identity matrix and all variability information about $\mathbf{p}$ is contained in the weights. This restricts the problem to a preferred-value approach to regularization, an approach different from that typically adopted when using pilot points in which prior information (in the form of preferred-difference (higher order Tikhonov) regularization) is often focused on the shape or structure of the $\mathbf{p}$ field without commitment to particular values. Nonetheless, this substitution is necessary for the equality to be obtained.

3. The weights assigned to the prior information must be equal to $\mathbf{C}_{pp}^{-1}$.

4. The weights assigned to the observations must be equal to $\mathbf{C}_{\varepsilon\varepsilon}^{-1}$.

5. The weights assigned to the prior information must be uncorrelated from the weights assigned to observations, as illustrated in equation 3.2.

If these conditions are all met, the OPR-PPR equation can be restated, recalling from above that $\mathbf{X}_{pri} = \mathbf{I}$, as

$$s^2\mathbf{y}^T \left(\mathbf{X}^T\mathbf{C}\mathbf{X}\right)^{-1}\mathbf{y} \;=\; s^2\mathbf{y}^T \left(\mathbf{X}_{obs}^T\mathbf{C}_{\varepsilon\varepsilon}^{-1}\mathbf{X}_{obs} + \mathbf{X}_{pri}^T\mathbf{C}_{pp}^{-1}\mathbf{X}_{pri}\right)^{-1}\mathbf{y} \tag{3.4}$$

$$=\; s^2\mathbf{y}^T \left(\mathbf{X}_{obs}^T\mathbf{C}_{\varepsilon\varepsilon}^{-1}\mathbf{X}_{obs} + \mathbf{C}_{pp}^{-1}\right)^{-1}\mathbf{y} \tag{3.5}$$

Then, using the following identity from Athans and Schweppe (1965, p. 31),

$$\left(\mathbf{X}_{11} - \mathbf{X}_{12}\mathbf{X}_{22}^{-1}\mathbf{X}_{21}\right)^{-1} = \mathbf{X}_{11}^{-1} + \mathbf{X}_{11}^{-1}\mathbf{X}_{12}\left(\mathbf{X}_{22} - \mathbf{X}_{21}\mathbf{X}_{11}^{-1}\mathbf{X}_{12}\right)^{-1}\mathbf{X}_{21}\mathbf{X}_{11}^{-1} \tag{3.6}$$

assigning

$$\mathbf{X}_{11} \;\equiv\; \mathbf{C}_{pp}^{-1} \tag{3.7}$$

$$\mathbf{X}_{21} \;\equiv\; -\mathbf{X} \tag{3.8}$$

$$\mathbf{X}_{12} \;\equiv\; -\mathbf{X}^T \tag{3.9}$$

$$\mathbf{X}_{22} \;\equiv\; -\mathbf{C}_{\varepsilon\varepsilon} \tag{3.10}$$

by substitution, and noting the distributive property with respect to multiplication by $\mathbf{y}$, we see

$$s^2\mathbf{y}^T \left(\mathbf{X}_{obs}^T\mathbf{C}_{\varepsilon\varepsilon}^{-1}\mathbf{X}_{obs} + \mathbf{C}_{pp}^{-1}\right)^{-1}\mathbf{y} = \mathbf{y}^T\mathbf{C}_{pp}\mathbf{y} - \mathbf{y}^T\mathbf{C}_{pp}\mathbf{X}_{obs}^T\left(\mathbf{X}_{obs}\mathbf{C}_{pp}\mathbf{X}_{obs}^T + \mathbf{C}_{\varepsilon\varepsilon}\right)^{-1}\mathbf{X}_{obs}\mathbf{C}_{pp}\mathbf{y} \tag{3.11}$$

It should be noted that the method described above is not fully documented in Tonkin and others (2007, 2008) or Poeter and others (2005). Making this extension to the code is therefore possible, but without supporting documentation and for the reasons given by Doherty and Hunt (2009), it is not recommended. Furthermore, it was our experience that under the current versions of UCODE_2005 and OPR-PPR, no more than 78 parameters could be evaluated—a limit of concern given the artifacts related to oversimplification demonstrated in this study. Revisions to both UCODE_2005 and OPR-PPR and their documentations are required to evaluate the same number of parameters as the PREDUNC software used here. The limitation is due, in part, to a conflict in the way sensitivity information is written by UCODE_2005 and read by OPR-PPR. This limitation does not arise unless a large number of parameters are used (greater than about 100). Nonetheless, both sides of equation 3.11 were tested for calculating data worth using data from the present problem in MATLAB Release R2008b (Mathworks, 2008) for both the overdetermined and underdetermined cases, and the results were identical (data not shown).

Note also that the two methods are not equal in terms of computational effort. The $\left(\mathbf{X}^T\mathbf{C}\mathbf{X}\right)^{-1}$ matrix for OPR-PPR has dimensions of $NPAR \times NPAR$, so as the number of parameters grows and exceeds the number of observations as in the underdetermined case, this matrix will become more difficult— or at high numbers of parameters, impossible—to invert. On the other hand, the matrix $\left(\mathbf{X}_{obs}\mathbf{C}_{pp}\mathbf{X}_{obs}^T + \mathbf{C}_{\varepsilon\varepsilon}\right)^{-1}$ that must be inverted for PREDUNC has dimensions of $NOBS \times NOBS$. This is most efficient in the underdetermined case, but in a strongly overdetermined context this method will perform somewhat more slowly. Ideally, depending on the dimensionality of the problem with respect to observations and parameters, the appropriate formulation could be chosen for the most computationally efficient outcome. PREDUNC has been revised to allow this option.

References

Athans, M., and Schweppe, F. C.,1965, Gradient matrices and matrix calculations: Lexington, Mass., Massachusetts Institute of Technology, Lincoln Laboratory Technical Note 1965-53, 34 p.

Doherty, J.E., and Hunt, R.J., 2009, Response to comment on "Two statistics for evaluating parameter identifiability and error reduction": Journal of Hydrology, v. 380, nos. 3–4, p. 489–496, doi:10.1016/j.jhydrol.2009.10.012.

Hill, M.C., and Tiedeman, C.R., 2007, Effective groundwater model calibration—with analysis of data, sensitivities, predictions, and uncertainty: Hoboken, N.J., Wiley-Interscience, 455 p.

Poeter, E.P., Hill, M.C., Banta, E.R., Mehl, Steffen, and Christensen, Steen, 2005, UCODE_2005 and six other computer codes for universal sensitivity analysis, calibration, and uncertainty—Evaluation version 1.015, Tech. rep., U. S. Geological Survey Techniques and Methods 6–A11, 283 p.

Tonkin, M.J., Tiedeman, C.R., Ely, M.D., and Hill, M.C., 2007, OPR-PPR, a computer program for assessing data importance to model predictions using linear statistics: U.S. Geological Survey Techniques and Methods 6–E2, 115 p.

Tonkin, M.J., Tiedeman, C.R., Ely, M.D., and Hill, M.C., 2008, Errata for OPR-PPR, a computer program for assessing data importance to model predictions using linear statistics: Errata to U.S. Geological Survey Techniques and Methods 6–E2, 1 p., accessed February 4, 2010, at *http://pubs.usgs.gov/tm/2007/tm6e2/pdf/tm_6-e2-errata.pdf.*

Appendix 4—Proof of the Athans and Schweppe Identity

The relation in equation 3.6 is key to evaluating the equivalence between OPR-PPR and PREDUNC under the specific conditions discussed in appendix 3. A proof is included here for completeness.

We start with the trivial identity

$$\mathbf{B}\mathbf{D}^{-1}\mathbf{B}^T\mathbf{A}^{-1}\mathbf{B} + \mathbf{B} = \mathbf{B}\mathbf{D}^{-1}\mathbf{B}^T\mathbf{A}^{-1}\mathbf{B} + \mathbf{B} \tag{4.1}$$

Now, using the following relations that are incumbent for invertible matrices (Strang, 1988, p. 42)

$$\mathbf{D}^{-1}\mathbf{D} = \mathbf{I} \text{ and } \mathbf{A}\mathbf{A}^{-1} = \mathbf{I} \tag{4.2}$$

we can substitute these two relations into equation 4.1

$$\mathbf{B}\mathbf{D}^{-1}\mathbf{B}^T\mathbf{A}^{-1}\mathbf{B} + \mathbf{B}\mathbf{D}^{-1}\mathbf{D} = \mathbf{B}\mathbf{D}^{-1}\mathbf{B}^T\mathbf{A}^{-1}\mathbf{B} + \mathbf{A}\mathbf{A}^{-1}\mathbf{B}. \tag{4.3}$$

This can be simplified to

$$\mathbf{B}\mathbf{D}^{-1}\left(\mathbf{B}^T\mathbf{A}^{-1}\mathbf{B} + \mathbf{D}\right) = \left(\mathbf{B}\mathbf{D}^{-1}\mathbf{B}^T + \mathbf{A}\right)\mathbf{A}^{-1}\mathbf{B}. \tag{4.4}$$

Now we premultiply both sides by $\left(\mathbf{B}\mathbf{D}^{-1}\mathbf{B}^T + \mathbf{A}\right)^{-1}$ and postmultiply both sides by $\left(\mathbf{B}^T\mathbf{A}^{-1}\mathbf{B} + \mathbf{D}\right)^{-1}$, leading to

$$\left(\mathbf{B}\mathbf{D}^{-1}\mathbf{B} + \mathbf{A}\right)^{-1}\mathbf{B}\mathbf{D}^{-1} = \mathbf{A}^{-1}\mathbf{B}\left(\mathbf{B}^{\mathbf{T}}\mathbf{A}^{-1}\mathbf{B} + \mathbf{D}\right)^{-1} \tag{4.5}$$

To bring this into terminology consistent with equation 3, we make the following substitutions

$$\mathbf{B} = \mathbf{X}_{obs}^T \tag{4.6}$$
$$\mathbf{D} = \mathbf{C}_{\varepsilon\varepsilon} \tag{4.7}$$
$$\mathbf{A} = \mathbf{C}_{pp}^{-1} \tag{4.8}$$

which result in

$$\left(\mathbf{X}_{obs}^T\mathbf{C}_{\varepsilon\varepsilon}^{-1}\mathbf{X}_{obs} + \mathbf{C}_{pp}^{-1}\right)^{-1}\mathbf{X}_{obs}^T\mathbf{C}_{\varepsilon\varepsilon}^{-1} = \mathbf{C}_{pp}\mathbf{X}_{obs}^T\left(\mathbf{X}_{obs}^T\mathbf{C}_{pp}\mathbf{X}_{obs} + \mathbf{C}_{\varepsilon\varepsilon}\right)^{-1} \tag{4.9}$$

From this point, it is easiest to start with the PREDUNC equation, apply the identity, and convert to the OPR-PPR equation. Starting with the right-hand side of equation 3.11, removing the prediction sensitivity ($\mathbf{y}$) and reference variance $\left(s^2\right)$ for clarity,

$$\mathbf{C}_{pp} - \mathbf{C}_{pp}\mathbf{X}_{obs}^T\left(\mathbf{X}_{obs}\mathbf{C}_{pp}\mathbf{X}_{obs}^T + \mathbf{C}_{\varepsilon\varepsilon}\right)^{-1}\mathbf{X}_{obs}\mathbf{C}_{pp} \tag{4.10}$$

Substituting in equation 4.9,

$$\mathbf{C}_{pp} - \left(\mathbf{X}_{obs}^T \mathbf{C}_{\varepsilon\varepsilon}^{-1} \mathbf{X}_{obs} + \mathbf{C}_{pp}^{-1}\right)^{-1} \mathbf{X}_{obs}^T \mathbf{C}_{\varepsilon\varepsilon}^{-1} \mathbf{X}_{obs} \mathbf{C}_{pp} \tag{4.11}$$

$$= \left[\mathbf{I} - \left(\mathbf{X}_{obs}^T \mathbf{C}_{\varepsilon\varepsilon}^{-1} \mathbf{X}_{obs} + \mathbf{C}_{pp}^{-1}\right)^{-1} \mathbf{X}_{obs}^T \mathbf{C}_{\varepsilon\varepsilon}^{-1} \mathbf{X}_{obs}\right] \mathbf{C}_{pp} \tag{4.12}$$

$$= \left[\begin{array}{c} \left(\mathbf{X}_{obs}^T \mathbf{C}_{\varepsilon\varepsilon}^{-1} \mathbf{X}_{obs} + \mathbf{C}_{pp}^{-1}\right)^{-1} \left(\mathbf{X}_{obs}^T \mathbf{C}_{\varepsilon\varepsilon}^{-1} \mathbf{X}_{obs} + \mathbf{C}_{pp}^{-1}\right) \\ - \left(\mathbf{X}_{obs}^T \mathbf{C}_{\varepsilon\varepsilon}^{-1} \mathbf{X}_{obs} + \mathbf{C}_{pp}^{-1}\right)^{-1} \mathbf{X}_{obs}^T \mathbf{C}_{\varepsilon\varepsilon}^{-1} \mathbf{X}_{obs} \end{array}\right] \mathbf{C}_{pp} \tag{4.13}$$

$$= \left[\left(\mathbf{X}_{obs}^T \mathbf{C}_{\varepsilon\varepsilon}^{-1} \mathbf{X}_{obs} + \mathbf{C}_{pp}^{-1}\right)^{-1} \left(\mathbf{X}_{obs}^T \mathbf{C}_{\varepsilon\varepsilon}^{-1} \mathbf{X}_{obs} + \mathbf{C}_{pp}^{-1}\right) - \mathbf{X}_{obs}^T \mathbf{C}_{\varepsilon\varepsilon}^{-1} \mathbf{X}_{obs}\right] \mathbf{C}_{pp} \tag{4.14}$$

$$= \left[\left(\mathbf{X}_{obs}^T \mathbf{C}_{\varepsilon\varepsilon}^{-1} \mathbf{X}_{obs} + \mathbf{C}_{pp}^{-1}\right)^{-1} \left(\mathbf{C}_{pp}^{-1}\right)\right] \mathbf{C}_{pp} \tag{4.15}$$

$$= \left(\mathbf{X}_{obs}^T \mathbf{C}_{\varepsilon\varepsilon}^{-1} \mathbf{X}_{obs} + \mathbf{C}_{pp}^{-1}\right)^{-1} \tag{4.16}$$

At this step, multiplying the prediction sensitivity $(\mathbf{y})$ and reference variance (s^2) back in, we are left with the left-hand side of equation 3.11

$$s^2 \mathbf{y}^T \left(\mathbf{X}_{obs}^T \mathbf{C}_{\varepsilon\varepsilon}^{-1} \mathbf{X}_{obs} + \mathbf{C}_{pp}^{-1}\right)^{-1} \mathbf{y} \tag{4.17}$$

References

Anderson, T.W., 1984, An introduction to multivariate statistical analysis (2d ed.): New York, Wiley, Wiley Series in Probability and Mathematical Statistics, 675 p.

Strang, Gilbert, 1988, Linear algebra and its applications (3d ed.): San Diego, Harcourt Brace Jovanovich, 505 p.